William Hodges

Travels in India, during the years 1780, 1781, 1782 & 1783

William Hodges

Travels in India, during the years 1780, 1781, 1782 & 1783

ISBN/EAN: 9783742844736

Manufactured in Europe, USA, Canada, Australia, Japa

Cover: Foto ©Andreas Hilbeck / pixelio.de

Manufactured and distributed by brebook publishing software (www.brebook.com)

William Hodges

Travels in India, during the years 1780, 1781, 1782 & 1783

TRAVELS
IN
INDIA,

DURING

THE YEARS

1780, 1781, 1782, & 1783.

BY WILLIAM HODGES, R. A.

===

LONDON:
PRINTED FOR THE AUTHOR,
AND SOLD BY J. EDWARDS, PALL-MALL.

MDCCXCIII.

TABLE of the PLATES,

WITH

DIRECTIONS TO THE BINDER.

		Engravers Names.
Pagoda at Tanjore, to face page	12	*Medland.*
Calcutta	14	*Byrne.*
Pafs at Sicri Gully	22	*Angus.*
Zananah	24	*Skelton.*
Banyan Tree	27	*Pouncy.*
Muffulman women, Moon-light	28	*Skelton.*
Peafant woman of Hindoftan, &c.	30	*Tompkins.*
Column	63	*Medland.*
Proceffion of a Hindoo woman to facrifice on the funeral pile	84	*Skelton.*
Bidjegur	86	*Pouncy.*
Palace at Lucknow	102	*Fittler.*
Agra	114	*Walker.*
Molhah, and Muffulman women	128	*Tompkins.*
Gwalior	142	*Byrne.*

LATELY PUBLISHED,

IN ONE VOLUME FOLIO, ATLAS SIZE,

Price 18l. in Sheets, or 20l. bound in Ruffia Leather,

A COLLECTION OF

VIEWS in INDIA,

DRAWN ON THE SPOT,

IN THE YEARS

1780, 1781, 1782, and 1783,

AND EXECUTED IN AQUATINTA, IN IMITATION OF THE ORIGINAL
DRAWINGS,

BY W. HODGES, R. A.

WITH HISTORICAL ACCOUNTS AND DESCRIPTIONS OF EACH.

PRINTED FOR THE AUTHOR,

AND SOLD BY J. EDWARDS, NO. 77, PALL-MALL.

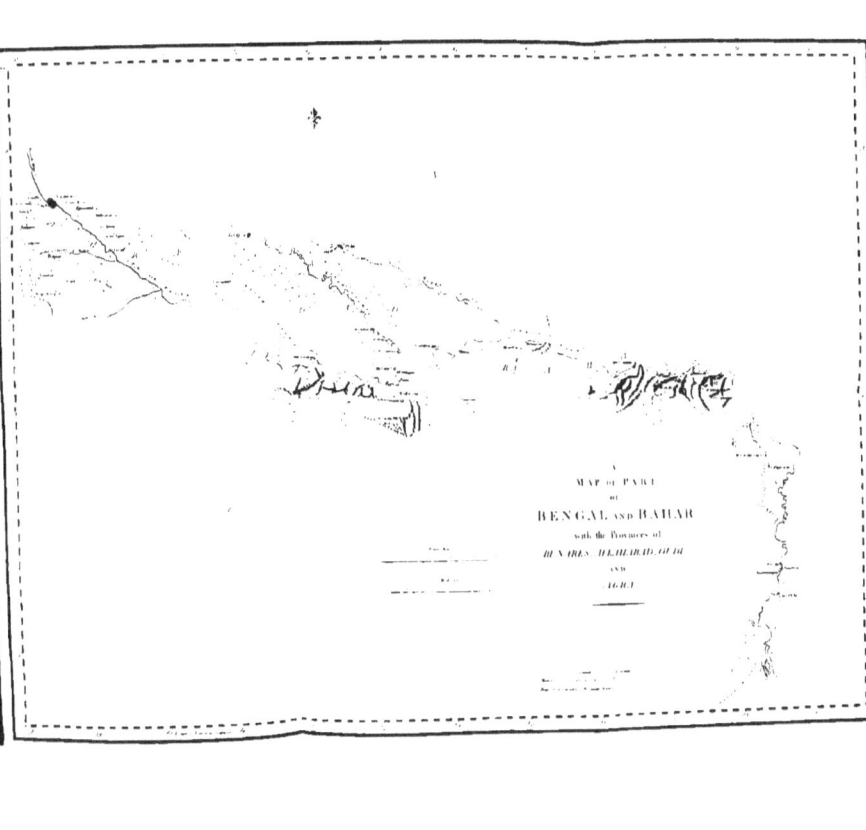

PREFACE.

THE intimate connexion which has so long subsisted between this country and the continent of India, naturally renders every Englishman deeply interested in all that relates to a quarter of the globe which has been the theatre of scenes highly important to his country; and which, perhaps, at the moment when he peruses the description of it, may be the residence or the grave of some of his dearest friends.

It is only matter of surprize, that, of a country so nearly allied to us, so little should be known. The public is, indeed, greatly indebted to the learned labours of gentlemen, who have resided there, for the information which they have afforded concerning the Laws and the Religion of the Hindoo tribes; as well as for correct and well digested details of the transactions of the Mogul government. But of the

PREFACE.

face of the country, of its arts, and natural productions, little has yet been said. Gentlemen who have resided long in India lose the idea of the first impression which that very curious country makes upon an entire stranger: the novelty is soon effaced, and the mind, by a common and natural operation, soon directs its views to more abstract speculation; reasoning assumes the place of observation, and the traveller is lost in the philosopher.

To supply, in some slight degree, this hiatus in the topographical department of literature, is the immediate object of the following pages. It will, I flatter myself, not be disagreeable to my readers to be informed, that they consist of a few plain observations, noted down upon the spot, in the simple garb of truth, without the smallest embellishment from fiction, or from fancy. They were chiefly intended for my own amusement, and to enable me to explain to my friends a number of drawings which I had made during my residence in India, some of which accompany the present publication. The apology is trite; but in this case its truth, and the respectability of the name to which I refer, must plead my excuse......it was owing entirely to the influence and persuasion of my most justly esteemed friend, Henry James Pye, Esq. Poet Laureat, that these observations have been submitted to a tribunal, which I have ever regarded with awful respect......THE PUBLIC.

PREFACE.   v.

WHILE I acknowledge my heart-felt obligations to one friend, it is not confiftent with my prefent feelings to omit the kind attentions of another. My learned friend, Dr. Gregory, by his perufal and revifion of my manufcript, contributed greatly to leffen my apprehenfions of that ordeal to which I was about to commit myfelf; and though he infifts upon my ftating, that his corrections were almoft entirely verbal, yet I cannot but be confcious, that, without them, the work would have appeared in a ftill more imperfect ftate.

AFTER all, I am aware that I ftand in need of every candid allowance on the part of my readers. It is evident that the ftudies abfolutely requifite to any degree of proficiency in a liberal art, and the practice of that art afterwards as a profeffion, can leave but little leifure for the cultivation of literature; and perhaps my engagements have been even more unfavourable to this object than thofe of moft artifts. A long circumnavigation, and the profeffional labour required in completing the works for Captain Cook's fecond voyage, occupied me for feveral years; and a voyage to India, with my different excurfions in that country, abforbed no inconfiderable portion of my time and attention.

ON another part of this work I can fpeak with rather more confidence, becaufe I am lefs perfonally concerned; and becaufe, as far as I am concerned, I appear in my proper profeffional character. The drawings, from which the plates for this work are engraved, I have already mentioned were made upon the fpot: and, to the utmoft of my ability, are fair and accurate reprefentations of the originals. Of the execution of the plates, while I feel that too much cannot be faid, my fenfes fufficiently convince me that it is unneceffary to fay any thing. I therefore conclude with fhortly returning my thanks to the artifts for the care and attention they have beftowed upon them.

QUEEN STREET, May Fair,
Feb. 18, 1793.

TRAVELS IN INDIA.

CHAP. I.

General Appearance of the Coast—Of the Town of Madras—Boats of the Country—First Reception of a Stranger—His Sensations on entering the Country—War with Hyder Ally—General Distress—Descriptive Sketch of the Country, Buildings, &c.—Indian Temple.

THE whole extent of the Coast of Coromandel is an even, low, sandy country; and about Madras the land rises so little and so gradually from the sea, that the spectator is scarcely able to mark the distinction, till he is assisted by the appearance of the different objects which present themselves upon the shore.

THE English town, rising from within Fort St. George, has from the sea a rich and beautiful appearance; the houses being covered with a stucco called chunam, which in itself is nearly as compact as the finest marble, and, as it bears as high a polish, is equally splendid with that elegant material. The stile of the buildings is in general handsome. They consist of long colonades, with open porticoes, and flat roofs, and offer to the eye an appearance similar to what we may conceive of a Grecian city in the age of Alexander. The clear, blue, cloudless sky, the polished white buildings, the bright sandy beach, and the dark green sea, present a combination totally new to the eye of an Englishman, just arrived from London, who, accustomed to the sight of rolling masses of clouds floating in a damp atmosphere, cannot but contemplate the difference with delight: and the eye being thus gratified, the mind soon assumes a gay and tranquil habit, analogous to the pleasing objects with which it is surrounded.

SOME time before the ship arrives at her anchoring ground, she is hailed by the boats of the country filled with people of business, who come in crowds on board. This is the moment in which an European feels the great distinction between Asia and his own country. The rustling of fine linen, and the general hum of unusual conversation, presents to his mind for a moment the idea of an assembly of females. When he ascends upon the deck,

he is ſtruck with the long muſlin dreſſes,* and black faces†
adorned with very large gold ear-rings and white turbans.
The firſt ſalutation he receives from theſe ſtrangers is by
bending their bodies very low, touching the deck with
the back of the hand, and the forehead three times.

THE natives firſt ſeen in India by an European voyager,
are Hindoos, the original inhabitants of the Peninſula.
In this part of India they are delicately framed, their
hands‡ in particular are more like thoſe of tender females; and do not appear to be, what is conſidered
a proper proportion to the reſt of the perſon, which is
uſually above the middle ſize. Correſpondent to this deli-

---

* THIS dreſs is in India uſually worn both by Hindoos and Mahomedans,
and is called Jammah; whence the dreſs well known in England, and worn
by children, is uſually called a jam.

† THE complexions of the people on the Coaſt of Coromandel and to the
ſouthward, are confiderably darker than thoſe to the northward. It is alſo to
be obſerved, that the native Hindoos are generally darker than the Muſ-
fulman, who originally came from Tartary and Perſia. The latter may
in fact be called a fair people; and I have even ſeen many of them with red
hair and florid complexions. It is a well known fact, that when a Tartar or
Perſian family has refided in India for a few generations, their complexions
have confiderably deepened. The Mogul family of the houſe of Timoor, I
underſtand, are of a deep olive complexion.

‡ IT has been obſerved of the arms frequently brought to this country, that
the gripe of the ſabre is too ſmall for moſt European hands.

cacy of appearance are their manners, mild, tranquil, and sedulously attentive: in this last respect they are indeed remarkable, as they never interrupt any person who is speaking, but wait patiently till he has concluded; and then answer with the most perfect respect and composure.

From the ship a stranger is conveyed on shore in a boat of the country, called a Massoolah boat: a work of curious construction, and well calculated to elude the violent shocks of the surf, that breaks here with great violence: they are formed without a keel, flat bottomed, with the sides raised high, and sewed together with the fibres of the cocoa-nut tree, and caulked with the same material: they are remarkably light, and are managed with great dexterity by the natives: they are usually attended by two kattamarans, (rafts) paddled by one man each, the intention of which is, that, should the boat be overset by the violence of the surf, the persons in it may be preserved. The boat is driven, as the sailors say, high and dry; and the passengers are landed on a fine, sandy beach: and immediately enter the fort of Madras.

The appearance of the natives is exceedingly varied, some are wholly naked, and others so clothed, that nothing but the face and neck is to be discovered; besides this, the European is struck at first with many other objects, such as women carried on men's shoulders on pallankeens, and men riding on horfeback clothed in linen dreffes like women: which, united with the very different face of the country from all he had ever feen or conceived of, excite the ftrongeft emotions of furprife!

It is impoffible to defcribe the enthufiafm with which I felt myfelf actuated on this occafion; all that I faw filled my mind with expectations of what was yet unfeen. I prepared therefore eagerly for a tour through the country; but my route was fcarcely fixed, when I was interrupted by the great fcourge of human nature, the great enemy of the arts, war, which, with horrors perhaps unknown to the civilized regions of Europe, defcended like a torrent over the whole face of the country, driving the peaceful hufbandman from his plow, and the manufacturer from his loom. On the eighteenth day of July, 1780, I was a melancholy witnefs to its effects, the multitude coming in from all quarters to Madras as a place of refuge, bearing on their fhoulders the fmall remains of their little property, mothers with infants at their breafts, fathers leading their horfes burthened with their young families, others fitting on the miferable remains of their fortunes on a hackery,* and dragged through the duft by weary bullocks: every object was marked by confufion and difmay, from the 18th to the 21ft, the numbers

---

* A hackery is a fmall covered carriage upon two wheels, drawn by bullocks, and ufed generally for the female part of the family.

daily increafing: and it was fuppofed that within the fpace of three days not lefs than two hundred thoufand of the country people were received within the *black town of Madras. Our Government behaved on this melancholy occafion with their ufual humanity and liberality; and not only publick, but private relief was afforded them to a confiderable amount.

THOSE poor people were foon afterwards diftributed to the northward, and into the fircars; which are lands that lay to the northward of Madras, and but of late years ceded to the Englifh Government.

MR. Smith was at this period at the head of the Government of Madras: and the folicitous attention of his lady, to relieve the private inconvenience of many Englifh families, who were alfo obliged to take fhelter within the walls of the fort, muft ever be remembered with refpect.

EVERY object that now prefented itfelf to the imagination bore the fame threatening and calamitous afpect: the country houfes of the Englifh, within one mile of the fort, were ftripped of their furniture, by the owners, even

---

* Adjoining the glacis of Fort St. George, to the northward, is a large town, commonly called the Black town, and which is fortified fufficiently to prevent any furprife by a body of horfe.

to the doors and window-blinds; this indeed was no more than necessary, as the enemy extended their depredations even to the walls of Madras; and no security could be found without the fort; until the camp was formed at the Mount, a place about ten English miles west of Madras. Every gentleman now possessing a house within the fort, was happy in accommodating the family of his friend; who before had resided on Choultry plain.*

THE troops being collected from different quarters, with provisions and a proper train of artillery, the vanquished spirits of the people appeared to revive; and the reyot was again seen cultivating his rice fields, or collecting the fruits. Nothing less was expected when the army took the field, but that Hyder Ally would very soon be escorted by a party of our troops into Fort St. George, and there make a public atonement for the miseries he had occasioned. This vision soon vanished, in the unhappy fate of Colonel Baillie's detachment, and the return

* THE country near Madras is a perfect flat, on which is built, at a small distance from the fort, a small Choultry: these are publick buildings found all over Hindostan, and are of Hindoo origin; they are in fact analogous to those buildings called caravanserais, well known through Asia. They have been erected and endowed by the liberality of princes, or the benevolence and piety of individuals. A Bramin generally attends them who administers relief to the poor and distressed, who are frequently supplied also with a matt to lie on, tanks, or reservoirs of water, or wells, are commonly near them.

of the army from a three week's campaign, reduced in its numbers and difpirited by its loffes. Thefe circumftances are too ftrongly marked in the page of hiftory to make it neceffary to recount their particulars in a defcriptive work like this. The arrival of Sir Eyre Coote from Bengal, with money and other fupplies, in September, and the active meafures purfued by that gallant officer, reftored confidence to the troops; and the moft fanguine hopes of the inhabitants from his exertions were not difappointed.

THE opportunities that offer to a painter are few, in a country which is over-run by an active enemy. I made however among others a drawing of Marmalong bridge, which is a very modern work, built, as I am informed, at the private expence of an Armenian merchant. It is over a fmall river that runs near the mount, and falls into the fea at a little diftance before the village of St. Thomá, four miles to the fouthward of Madras. The Portugueze had formerly a confiderable fettlement at this village. The church and the dwelling-houfes of a few Portugueze families yet remain here. The legendary tale of the Roman Catholic church is, that St. Thomas the apoftle, in the courfe of his miffion to India, fuffered martyrdom on the fpot where the church is built.

THE fettlement of Madras was formed by the Englifh at or about the middle of the laft century, and was a place of no real confequence, but for its trade, until the war fo ably carried on by General Stringer Lawrence, from the years 1748 to 1752; and which originated from the claims of Chunda Saib, in oppofition to our ally Mahomed Ally Cawn, the prefent Nabob of Arcot; from which period the Englifh may be confidered as Sovereigns. In the fchool of this able officer the late Lord Clive received his military education.

FORT St. George, or Madras, rifes, as has been already intimated, from the margin of the fea, and is allowed by the ableft engineers to be a place of confiderable ftrength. It was planned by the ingenious Mr. Robins, the author of Lord Anfon's Voyages, who was eminent for his general and philofophical, as well as for his mathematical knowledge. Since his time many works have been added.

IN Fort St. George are many handfome and fpacious ftreets. The houfes may be confidered as elegant, and particularly fo from the beautiful material with which they are finifhed, the chunam. The inner apartments are not highly decorated, prefenting to the eye only white walls; which, however, from the marble-like appearance of the ftucco, give a frefhnefs grateful in fo hot a country. Ceilings are very uncommon in the rooms. Indeed it is impoffible to find any which will refift the ravages of that deftructive infect the white ant. Thefe animals are chiefly formidable from the immenfity of their numbers, which are fuch as to deftroy, in one night's time, a ceiling of any dimenfions. I faw an inftance in the ceiling to the portico of the Admiralty, or Governor's houfe, which fell in flakes of twenty feet fquare. It is the wood work which ferves for the bafis of the ceilings, fuch as the laths, beams, &c. that thefe infects attack; and this will ferve to explain the circumftance I have juft mentioned.

THE houfes on Choultry plain are many of them beautiful pieces of architecture, the apartments fpacious and magnificent. I know not that I ever felt more delight, than in going on a vifit to a family on Choultry plain, foon after my arrival at Madras, in the cool of the evening, after a very hot day. The moon fhone in its fulleft luftre, not a cloud overcaft the fky, and every houfe on the plain was illuminated. Each family, with their friends, were in the open porticoes, enjoying the breeze. Such a fcene appears more like a tale of enchantment than a reality, to the imagination of a ftranger juft arrived.

THERE are few objects to be met with here, which ferve to illuftrate the hiftory or characters of the original inhabitants of India. One, however, is too curious to be omitted, and that is a beautiful Hindoo Temple, or Pagoda, at Triplecane, two miles fouth of Madras. It is of confiderable magnitude; and the top of the building rifing confiderably above the trees, it is feen all over the country. Adjoining to the temple is a large tank, with fteps defcending to the bottom, filled with water. The whole is of ftone, and the mafonry excellent. On the furface of the temple are many baffo relievos, which I fuppofe to relate to the religion of the Hindoos; but whether they are connected with the rites and worfhip of Bramah or not, I am not able to fay: for fome of them are of the moft indecent kind. I made an accurate drawing of this building, which was fent to England, and loft on board the General Barker Eaft Indiaman, when that fhip was wrecked on the coaft of Holland, in 1781; but as I have made drawings of other Hindoo temples, I lefs lament the lofs. The annexed plate, a view of the great Pagoda at Tanjore, is from a picture which I painted from an accurate drawing made by Mr. Topping, an ingenious friend of mine, now on a furvey of the coaft of Coromandel for the Hon. the Eaft India Company, and will ferve to give the reader a general idea of thefe efforts of Indian architecture.

A VIEW of the GREAT PAGODA at TANJORE.

CHAP. II.

Voyage to Bengal—Defcription of the Fort and Town of Calcutta—Route from Calcutta to the Plains of Plaffey—Defcription of that memorable Spot—The Author's Progrefs through the Country—Ruins of a Zananah—Cataract of Mootejerna—Happinefs of India—Defcription of Bauglepoor —Town and Fort of Mongheir—Remarks on the Mode of travelling in India—Voyage back to Calcutta on the Ganges— Temples—Females bathing—Singular Appearance by Night.

AFTER refiding a year at Madras, as no profpect prefented itfelf of feeing and making drawings in the interior part of the country, I determined to purfue my voyage to Bengal: and as I found my health on the decline, I entertained thoughts of returning to Europe by the following feafon. I embarked in February, 1781, and arrived in the Ganges in March. A change of air and a fea voyage frequently produces a happy alteration in the conftitutions of valetudinarians in India; and I accordingly found that on my arrival in Bengal my health was perfectly re-eftablifhed.

THE appearance of the country on the entrance of the Ganges, or Houghly River (this being only a branch of the

Great Ganges) is rather unpromifing; a few bufhes at the water's edge, forming a dark line, juft marking the diftinction between fky and water, are the only objects to be feen. As the fhip approaches Calcutta the river narrows; that which is called the Garden Reach, prefents a view of handfome buildings, on a flat furrounded by gardens: thefe are villas belonging to the opulent inhabitants of Calcutta. The veffel has no fooner gained one other reach of the river than the whole city of Calcutta burfts upon the eye. This capital of the Britifh dominions in the Eaft is marked by a confiderable fortrefs, on the fouth fide of the river, which is allowed to be, in ftrength and correctnefs of defign, fuperior to any in India. On the fore ground of the picture is the water-gate of the fort, which reflects great honour on the talents of the engineer—the ingenious Colonel Polier. The glacis and efplanade are feen in perfpective, bounded by a range of beautiful and regular buildings; and a confiderable reach of the river, with veffels of various claffes and fizes, from the largeft Indiamen to the fmalleft boat of the country, clofes the fcene. A plate, reprefenting this view, from a picture taken on the fpot, and admirably engraved by Mr. Byrne, an artift whofe reputation is not to be raifed by any eulogium in this place, is annexed.

A EUROPEAN lands here in the midft of a great city, without paffing the outer draw-bridges of a fort: here are no centinels with the keen eye of fufpicion, no ftoppage of

baggage. The hofpitality which a ftranger experiences from the inhabitants, and particularly from thofe to whom he is recommended, correfponds exactly with the freedom of his admiffion into the city; and the kindnefs which I experienced on this occafion from my much lamented friend Henry Davies, Efq. late Advocate General of Bengal, can never be forgotten.

THE city of Calcutta extends from the Weftern point of Fort William, along the banks of the river, almoft to the village of Coffipoor: that is about four and a half Englifh miles. The breadth in many parts is inconfiderable. The ftreets are broad; the line of buildings, furrounding two fides of the efplanade of the fort, is magnificent; and it adds greatly to the fuperb appearance, that the houfes are detached from each other, and infulated in a great fpace. The buildings are all on a large fcale, from the neceffity of having a free circulation of air, in a climate the heat of which is extreme. The general approach to the houfes is by a flight of fteps, with great projecting porticoes, or furrounded by colonades or arcades, which give them the appearance of Grecian temples; and indeed every houfe may be confidered as a temple dedicated to hofpitality.

CALCUTTA, from a fmall and inconfiderable fort, which yet remains (and in which is the famous black-hole, fo fatal to many of our countrymen in 1756), and a few warehouses, was soon raised to a great and opulent city, when the government of the kingdom of Bengal fell into the hands of the English. For its magnificence, however, it is indebted solely to the liberal spirit and excellent taste of the late Governor General; and it must be confessed, that the first house was raised by Mr. Hastings which deserves the name of a piece of architecture: in fact, it is even in a purer style than any that has been built since, although it is on a smaller scale than many others.

THE mixture of European and Asiatic manners, which may be observed in Calcutta, is curious:—coaches, phætons, single horse chaises, with the pallankeens and hackeries of the natives—the passing ceremonies of the Hindoos—the different appearances of the fakirs—form a sight perhaps more novel and extraordinary than any city in the world can present to a stranger. Some views in the city of Calcutta, published by Mr. Daniel, are highly to be commended for their accuracy.

A FEW weeks after my arrival in Bengal, an opportunity offered itself, which I immediately embraced, to make drawings of part of the country, as high as Mongheir, on the Ganges, a distance of three hundred English miles; and I proceeded on this journey in the middle of the month of April following, by dauk bearers (in a pallankeen) or pallankeen carriers. These are persons hired by government, and fixed at the several stages or posts for facilitating travelling: each stage, on an average, may be ten English miles. The number of persons are usually nine, with two additional men or boys, to carry baggage and lights in the night, called mossoljees, from the name of the lights, mossol.

From the apparent state of a country, a just estimate may generally be formed of the happiness or the misery of a people. Where there is neatness in the cultivation of the land, and that land tilled to the utmost of its boundaries, it may reasonably be supposed that the government is the protector and not the oppressor of the people. Throughout the kingdom of Bengal it appears highly flourishing in tillage of every kind, and abounding in cattle. The villages are neat and clean, and filled with swarms of people.

There are few objects to attract the attention of the curious traveller from Calcutta, until he reaches the plains of Plassey. This spot to every reflecting Englishman must be highly interesting, when he considers that on this theatre, in the month of June, 1757, was disputed the existence of his countrymen in Bengal, even as merchants. The great abilities displayed by Lord Clive previous to the battle of Plassey, as well as in that action, both as a general and a politician, undoubtedly entitle him to the high reputation which is attached to his memory; since on that plain was laid the foundation of an empire in India, the influence of which has extended over a larger tract of country, and greater numbers of people, than have been united under any one government since the time of Aurungzebe.

At Plassey is a house which was once a hunting seat of the Nabob of Bengal: it is distant from Calcutta about seventy English miles, and somewhat more than thirty from Moorshedabad. In Moorshedabad there are few buildings of note: the most considerable is the remains of the Cutterah. This was formerly a publick seminary for men of learning among the Musselmans; but it has long since gone to decay. It consists of a large square area, each side of which is somewhat more than seventy feet in length, surrounded by a cloyster, divided into single rooms, crowned with a dome, and one window in each. In the center on the side opposite the entrance was a mosque, raised considerably above the buildings on either side: the extreme angles on that side where the mosque was situated are terminated by two towers, rising several feet higher than the rest of the building.

This building was erected by Jaffier Cawn, the Nabob of Bengal, in the early part of the present century; who, from the mildness of his manners, his love of learning, and strict attention to justice, was the most popular nobleman who ever held that office in Bengal under the Mogul government. Moorshedabad was the seat of his residence,

INDIA.

and to this place he invited men of talents. On the opposite side of the river is the tomb of Aliverdi Cawn, the grandfather of Suraja Dowlah, so well known for his hatred to the English, and his conduct to his prisoners on the taking of Calcutta in 1756.* This is an oblong building,

* When the fort of Calcutta was closely besieged by Suraja Dowlah, Mr. Drake, the governor, and many others, with several ladies of the settlement, escaped to the English ships then lying off the town, and which ships fell down as low as Fulta, one third of the distance to the mouth of the river, where they remained for seven months in the greatest distress, both for provisions and every other article of necessaries. Mr. Gregory, a gentleman since well known in the political world, and particularly for his knowledge in India affairs, and many years a Director of the East India Company in London, ventured in a very heavy gale of wind, in a country boat, to pass Calcutta, and proceeded to Chardenagore, to solicit assistance from the French governor, who received him with all the personal politeness that is the mark of that nation, but without offering any thing to remove the distress of the English at Fulta. From the French Mr. Gregory proceeded to the Dutch settlement at Chinsurah, where he was received with unaffected good manners and friendliness. After relating the distresses his countrymen laboured under, the Dutch governor prepared for their relief; and his lady went round the settlement and procured linen and other articles, for the accommodation and comfort of the ladies; and, in the course of two days, the governor dispatched a sloop, under the care of Mr. Van Staten, their commander in chief, to the English, loaded with several articles of provisions, many chests of wine, and twenty leaguers of arrack, for the use of the people. At the same time this humanity was shewn to the people on board the ships, the governor's house was so filled with the distressed that had escaped from Calcutta, that he and his family were obliged to sleep on board a budgerow in the river. The name of the Dutch governor, Mr. Adrian Bisdam, must ever be remembered by the English with respect.

crowned with five domes; the center one much larger than the others, and the two extremes lefs than the intermediate. This pyramidal form is ufual in all the buildings of the Eaft, whether Moorifh or Hindoo: fo minutely attentive have they been to this, that a mofque at Chunar, being tried with a cord ftretched from the fummit of the center building, the cord has been found to touch the extremes at the outer wall that inclofes the building. During the ufurpation of Aliverdi Cawn, his wars with the Marhattas, who were continually over-running the country, left him little leifure for the embellifhment of the city, however he might have been difpofed.

THE road proceeds from Moorfhedabad through the villages of Jungepoor and Sooty, to Oodooanullah. This road is croffed by feveral nullahs,† fome of which have ferry boats ftationed at them, to accommodate the traveller. At the laft mentioned place is a bridge, built by Sultan Sujah, the fecond fon of the Emperor Shah Iehan,* who was appointed Subah of the province of Bengal, one hundred and thirty years ago. This is one of the moft elegant fpecimens in architecture of thofe times; and it has become famous in ours by the victory obtained over the troops of Meer Coffim, in the year 1764, by the late Major Adams. This

† Nullahs are fmall ftreams, or brooks.

* The Emperor Shah Iehan began his reign in the year 1627, and reigned thirty-two years. He was depofed by his third fon, the famous Allumgire; better known in Europe by the name of Aurungzebe.

victory was facilitated by an accident that happened on the bridge: the carriage of one of the enemy's large pieces of artillery broke down, and ſtopping the retreat, threw them into confuſion. Oodooanullah is two miles from Rajemahel; and Rajemahel is nearly eighty miles from Moorſhedabad: it lies on the weſtern bank of the Ganges, which is high and bold, and at the foot of a chain of hills. The ſituation is eſteemed unhealthy, from the foreſts in its neighbourhood. It was the ſeat of the government of Bengal, under Sultan Sujah, and it continued to be his reſidence until he fell in the conteſt for the empire with his brother Aurungzebe. The numberleſs ruins found at and in the neighbourhood, evinced his paſſion for building; and the great extent of many of them affords a proof of his ſplendor and magnificence. There yet remains a part of the palace: which was ſupported by vaſt octangular piers, raiſed from the edge of the river. The great hall yet remains, with ſome leſſer apartments, as well as the principal gate leading to the palace: theſe are ſurrounded by immenſe maſſes of ruins. This palace, in the time of Sultan Sujah, was nearly deſtroyed by fire: the zananah, or that part inhabited by the females of his family, was totally deſtroyed.

A TRADITION prevails in this part of the country, that more than three hundred women fell a ſacrifice to modeſty on this occaſion; none of them daring to ſave themſelves, from the apprehenſion of being ſeen by the men. At a little diſtance from Rajemahel are the ruins of a zananah, which I went from curioſity to inſpect, as they are when inhabited ſacred places; and I was gratified extremely to obſerve the perfect accuracy in the Hindoſtan pictures which repreſent them. The annexed plate is from an old picture of one which I met with in India. It may not be improper to remark, while I am upon this ſubject, that when the Mogul government was in the plenitude of its power, it was an object with the Omrahs, or great Lords of the court, to hold captive in their zananahs even hundreds of females, collected from various quarters of the empire, and particularly ſo from Caſhmire, a country famous for the beauty of its women.* From Rajemahel the publick road continues by the ſide of the river, at the foot of the hills, to the paſs of Sicri Gully, whence it enters the province of Bahar. This paſs, in the time of the Hindoo and Mogul governments was the commanding entrance from Bahar into the kingdom of Bengal, and was formerly fortified with a ſtrong wall and gate, the ruins of which yet remain. What muſt ſhew the inutility of ſuch fortifications, and the wiſdom of the Britiſh government in ſuffering them to go to

* I cannot but here obſerve that, from the cloſe confinement of the Mahomedan women, there reigns in the zananahs a refined ſpirit of intrigue unknown in Europe in the preſent day. Many accounts are to be found of ſuch in the old Spaniſh novels, which may be accounted for from the Spaniards retaining cuſtoms and prejudices eſtabliſhed among them by their Mooriſh conquerors, long after their expulſion in the fifteenth century.

THE PASS of SICRI GULLY from BENGAL entering into the Province of BAHAR.

decay, is the ease with which they are eluded; for, in the year 1742-3, the whole Mahratta army, consisting of fifty thousand men, under Bofchow Pundit, passed through the hills above Colgong, and to the south-west of this pass into Bengal. On the top of the hill is a ruined tomb of a Muffulman sied, or saint. The whole scene appeared to me highly picturesque; a plate, therefore, is given of this view, as it marks the general character of this part of the country. At this place I was met by a party of seapoys, sent by my much lamented and revered friend, the late Augustus Cleveland, Esq. then collector of the districts of Rajemahel and Bauglepoor, to escort me to the falls of Mootejerna in the hills, about four cofs, or eight English miles inland from the river. From the height of the hills, these cascades are clearly seen, in the time of the rains, the river being then near thirty feet higher than in the dry season, and the falls considerably increased. The road, or rather path, is through the jungles, or woods; and when rain has lately fallen in the hills, the noise of the cataract is distinctly heard at the distance of two English miles. It consists of two falls, which taken together, the perpendicular height measures one hundred and five feet. The water, falling over vast masses of rocks, is received in a bason below, and continues running through fragments of the rock, rent from above, until it is lost in the Ganges. At the bottom of the lower fall is a great hollow cave, which is easily entered from either side, and the water is seen from within, forming part of the arc of a great circle before. In the interior part of this cave, which may be thirty feet from the front of the rock, the base appears to be a mixture of rock and charcoal; that is, the interstices of the rock appear filled with charcoal, and many fragments broken off are composed equally of the two materials. For the satisfaction of others I brought away with me two large pieces, which I afterwards shewed to several ingenious gentlemen in Calcutta. The place itself, it is true, is held in superstitious veneration by the common people of the country; and it is possible some religious ceremonies may have passed here, but it is scarcely probable that any fire used in such ceremonies could have produced such effects.

AFTER returning to Sicri Gully, I continued my route acrofs the pafs of Terriagully, from the top of which a beautiful scene opens itself to the view; namely, the meandering of the river Ganges through the flat country, and glittering through an immense plain, highly cultivated, as far as the extent of the horizon, where the eye is almost at a loss to discriminate the termination of sky and land. From the pass of Terriagully the road continues by the river side, opening in extensive glades, covered with a fine turf, and only interfperfed with woods, confifting of timber trees of confiderable magnitude, which, from the great heat and moisture in this part of India, (like all other vegetable productions of the country) continue verdant through a great part of the year. After this the road skirts the woods, and

A VIEW of the INSIDE of A ZANANAH.

Engraved by W. Skelton from an Indian Painting
in the possession of William Hodges R.A.

London, Published by J. Edwards, Pall Mall, June 1st, 1794.

under great trees, which are filled with a variety of birds of beautiful colours, many of them of the parrot tribe; and, amongst others, peacocks in abundance, which fitting on the vast horizontal branches, and difplaying their varied plumage to the fun, dazzle the eyes of the traveller as he paffes. In this route many inferior rivers are paffed, that feed the waters of the Great Ganges, which, at this feafon of the year, are very low; and the fteepnefs of many of their banks renders the carriage extremely troublefome to the pallankeen bearers. At Colgong there is a confiderable ftream, that falls into the Ganges, which by its continued force, and particularly in the time of the periodical rains, has detached two large rocks, and formed them into iflands, covered with woods, full feventy yards from the fhore. There is a paffage between the iflands and the fhore filled with funken rocks, which form violent eddies. The paffage is fometimes only to be effected by fmall boats; and in the time of the rains is efteemed exceedingly dangerous. I knew an inftance in which it had nearly proved fatal.

THE country about Colgong is, I think, the moft beautiful I have feen in India. The waving appearance of the land, its fine turf and detached woods, backed by the extenfive forefts on the hills, brought to my mind many of the fine parks in England; and its overlooking the Ganges, which has more the appearance of an ocean at this place than of a river, gives the profpect inexpreffible grandeur.

From this place my route was continued to the village of Sultungunge; oppofite to which, in the river, is the fmall ifland of Jangerah, or, according to fome authors, Jehangueery. This ifland is a rock, with a few trees growing from its interftices, and on the top is a fmall hermitage, inhabited by a Hindoo monk. The fituation this holy father has chofen is certainly a proof of his tafte and of his judgment; for, from the top, he has a moft extenfive profpect of the country and river; and in the fummer heats it muft be cooler than any fituation in its neighbourhood. This rock is confidered by the Hindoos as a facred place; and on many parts of it are pieces of fculpture relative to their mythology. I am concerned I cannot pay fo high a compliment to the art of fculpture among the Hindoos as is ufually paid by many ingenious authors who write on the religion of Bramah. Confidering thefe works, as I do, with the eyes of an artift, they are only to be paralleled with the rude effays of the ingenious Indians I have met with in Otaheite, and on other iflands in the South Seas. The time when thefe fculptures were produced I believe is not eafy to afcertain; but thus much is certain, that the more modern works in fculpture of human figures, by the Hindoos, lay claim to very little more merit than the ancient productions. Some ornaments, however, that I have feen on

BANYAN TREE.

Hindoo temples are beautifully carved: but of this I shall have occasion to speak hereafter, when I treat of the subject of Hindoo architecture.

I PROCEEDED from Sultungunge to Bauglepoor, where my pursuits were promoted with a degree of liberality that peculiarly marked the mind of the gentleman who then governed this district; and of whom, in common gratitude, I must ever speak with veneration and esteem. At the entrance of the town of Bauglepoor, I made a drawing of a banyan tree, of which a plate is annexed. This is one of those curious productions in nature which cannot fail to excite the attention of the traveller. The branches of this tree having shoots depending from them, and taking root, again produce, and become the parents of others. These trees, in many instances, cover such an extent of ground, that hundreds of people may take shelter under one of them from the scorching rays of the sun. The care that was taken in the government, and the minute attention to the happiness of the people, rendered this district, at this time, (1781) a perfect paradise. It was not uncommon to see the manufacturer at his loom, in the cool shade, attended by his friend softening his labour by the tender strains of music. There are to be met with in India many old pictures representing similar subjects, in the happy times of the Mogul government.

THE situation of the Resident's house, built by Mr. Cleveland, is on a very elevated spot: it is on the banks of a nullah, forming a large island, bounded by the Ganges on one side, and the nullah encircling the other: the island is about four miles across. On the other side is a beautiful park-like country, with clumps of great trees, separated by glades; the whole bounded by wood. This place owes its principal beauty to the good taste of Mr. Cleveland.

FROM Bauglepoor to Mongheir, is between thirty and forty English miles. The roads are good, the country highly cultivated, and the villages neat. Along the side of the road are the burial places of the Mussulmans; for they, like the ancient Greeks, always bury by or near the highways: those of the common people are mounds of earth, covering the whole length of the body, with a small square column at the head, about three feet high, and another, not more than eighteen inches, at the feet: those of superior rank have mausoleums, decorated in proportion to the wealth or munificence of the family. It is a custom with the women of the family to attend these tombs of their friends, or nearest and most valued relations, after sun-set; and it is both affecting and curious to see them proceeding in groups, carrying lamps in their hands, which they place at the head of the tomb: the effect, considered in a picturesque light, is highly beautiful; with that of sentiment, it is delightful. A print of this subject is subjoined.

MAHOMMEDAN WOMEN attending the TOMBS of their Parents, Relatives, or Friends, at NIGHT.

MONGHEIR is a large Indian town, with an old fort. One fide of the fort is flanked by the Ganges, and that to the land by a wide and deep ditch. There are three principal gates; one on the fide next the river, another on the eaft fide, and another on the fouth. That to the eaft appears to have been very ftrong: the walls are flanked with fquare towers, in the old ftile of caftles; many fimilar ruins being now to be found in England. The fort was built in the middle of the laft century, by Sultan Sujah; but the place is famous for being a military ftation many centuries back.* The area within the walls of the fort is very confiderable; it is generally made a ftation for a part of the Englifh troops; and there is a houfe here for the commanding officer, built by the late General Goddard.

FROM Calcutta to Mongheir the face of the country is extremely varied. Bengal, however, to the entrance into the province of Bahar, is almoft a perfect flat, or the rife is fo gentle as not to be perceived. The foil is rich, confifting chiefly of a black earth, intermixt with fine fand. From Rajemahel it affumes a different character; hills are feen rifing in many parts into mountains, and covered with immenfe forefts of timber: the foil here is alfo more arid, and the air drier, than in the lower parts of Bengal. The heat

* On this fpot was found, a few years back, a brafs plate, with a Sanfchrite infcription of a grant, as early as the firft century of Chriftianity.

in the months of March, April, and May, is immoderate; and, until it becomes tempered by the rains that conſtantly fall in June and July, it is dreadful to the bearers of the pallankeens to travel in the middle of the day: the duſt and heat are then, indeed, ſo intolerable, that they are frequently under the neceſſity of putting down their burthens, and ſheltering themſelves beneath the ſhade of the banyan trees, many of which are found on the road, particularly by the ſide of wells, or ſome little choultry on the borders of a tank. The number of theſe rural accommodations for travellers reflect the higheſt credit on the care of the old Hindoo and Mooriſh governments. It is particularly mentioned in the life of the Emperor Shere Shah, that, although a uſurper who obtained the empire by the moſt atrocious acts, he paid the moſt humane attention to the comforts and accommodations of his people. He cauſed wells to be dug at every coſs, (or two miles) and trees to be planted on the road ſide. At many of theſe wells have I halted in my journies. They are, in general, from ten to fourteen feet in diameter, and lined with ſtone: the maſonry excellent; and they are raiſed from the ſurface of the ground by a little wall two feet high. I ſhould have remarked that, throughout Bengal and Bahar, the water is excellent. It is extremely pleaſant to obſerve the variety of travellers that are to be met with on the road; either paſſing along in groups, under the ſhade of ſome ſpreading tree, by the ſide of the wells or tanks. In one part may be ſeen the native ſoldiers, their half pikes ſticking

A PEASANT WOMAN of HINDOSTAN.   A SEPOY MATCHLOCK MAN, in the Service of the native PRINCES of HINDOSTAN.

Drawn from the Life by W. Hodges R.A.

London, Published by J. Edwards, Pall Mall, Jan.r 1, 1793.

by their fide, and their fhields lying by them, with their fabres and matchlocks; in another part is, perhaps, a company of merchants, engaged in calculation, or of devotees in the act of focial worfhip; and in another, the common Hindoo pallankeen bearers baking their bread. This operation is performed in an eafy and expeditious manner by thefe people: they make a fmall hole in the earth of about a foot in diameter, in which they light a fire, and on the top of the fire they place a flat iron plate, which they always carry with them, and which they fupport with ftones; they mix their flour with a little water, and bake their cakes, which are foon dreffed, are very wholefome, and I think not unpalatable. On the whole, I muft fay, that the fimplicity and primitive appearance of thefe groups delighted me.

It is not uncommon alfo, in excurfions through thefe parts of the country, to meet with various fakirs, with a more than favage appearance. Sometimes whole families may be feen travelling up and down the country, forming moft beautiful picturefque groups; fometimes with camels loaded with goods; fome of the party riding on bullocks, the females in hackeries, and the younger part of the company on fmall horfes, brought from the mountains bordering the eaftern fide of Bengal. Thefe horfes are called tanyans, and are moftly pye-bald. The men march on foot, armed with fpears and matchlocks: their fabres and fhields are flung acrofs their backs. Thefe are certainly valuable fubjects for the painter. The lodgings of the traveller in India are the ferais, or caravanferais, (or places for the caravans) as they are called in Europe. Many of thefe are in the great roads, and have been erected either by charitable perfons, or at the public expence. The Emperor, whom I have already mentioned for his attention to the public accommodation, built many, from the extremity of Bengal to Lahore. There is a noble building of this kind remaining at Rajemahel, built by Sultan Sujah, when Subah of Bengal. The form is a fquare of equal fides; the entrance from the Bengal road is through a large and highly ornamented gate, which alfo poffeffes military ftrength no lefs than beauty. Round the four fides is a wall about twenty feet high; attached to the wall round the fides are feparate apartments, covered on the top, and open to the center of the area within. In thefe places the traveller lodges his goods, and fleeps; the area within the fquare is for the beafts. Attendant on thefe ferais are poor people, who furnifh a fmall bedftead for the traveller to fleep on, and who are rewarded by a trifling fum, amounting to perhaps a penny Englifh. The Mahomedan is, in general, a generous man compared with the Hindoo on thefe occafions. Oppofite the Bengal gate is another in this ferai; which, however, is nothing more than merely an opening through the wall.

FROM Mongheir I embarked, and returned by water to Calcutta; and here I had an opportunity of obferving a feries of scenery perfectly new; the different boats of the country, and the varied shores of the Ganges. This immense current of water suggests rather the idea of an ocean than of a river, the general breadth of it being from two to five miles, and in some places more. The largest boats sailing up or passing down, appear, when in the middle of the stream, as mere points, and the eastern shore only as a dark line marking the horizon. The rivers I have seen in Europe, even the Rhine, appear as rivulets in comparison with this enormous mass of water. I do not know a more pleasant amusement than sailing down the Ganges in the warm season: the air, passing over the great reaches of the river many miles in length, is so tempered as to feel delightfully refreshing. After sun-set the boats are generally moored close to the banks, where the shore is bold, and near a gunge or market, for the accommodation of the people. It is common, on the banks of the river, to see small Hindoo temples, with gauts or passages, and flights of steps to the river. In the mornings, at or after sun-rise, the women bathe in the river; and the younger part, in particular, continue a considerable time in the water, sporting and playing like Naiads or Syrens. To a painter's mind, the fine antique figures never fail to present themselves, when he observes a beautiful female form ascending these steps from the river, with wet drapery, which perfectly displays the whole person, and with vases on their heads, carrying water to the temples. A sight no less novel or extraordinary, is the Bramins at their oraifons; perfectly abstracted, for the time, to every paffing object, however attractive. Thefe devotees are generally naked, except a fmall piece of drapery round the middle. A furprizing fpirit of cleanlinefs is to be obferved among the Hindoos: the streets of their villages are commonly fwept and watered, and fand is frequently strewed before the doors of the houfes. The fimplicity, and perfectly modest character, of the Hindoo women, cannot but arrest the attention of a stranger. With downcast eye, and equal step, they proceed along, and fcarcely turn to the right or to the left to obferve a foreigner as he paffes, however new or fingular his appearance. The men are no lefs remarkable for their hofpitality, and are constantly attentive to accommodate the traveller in his wants. During the whole of the journey in my pallankeen, whatever I wanted, as boiling water for my tea, milk, eggs, &c. &c. I never met with impofition or delay, but always experienced an uncommon readinefs to oblige, and that accompanied with manners the most fimple and accommodating. In perfect oppofition is the Muffulman character;—haughty, not to fay infolent; irritable, and ferocious. I beg, however, to be underflood of the lower claffes; for a Moorifh gentleman may be confidered as a perfect model of a well bred man. The Hindoos are chiefly hufbandmen, manufacturers, and merchants, except two tribes—the Rajapoots, who are military, and the Bramins, who are ecclefiastics. The Muffulmans may be claffed as entirely military, as few of them exercife any other employment, except collecting the revenues, which under the Moorish governments have been always done by military force.

At this season of the year it is not uncommon, towards the evening, to see a small black cloud rising in the eastern part of the horizon, and afterwards spreading itself to the north-west. This phenomenon is always attended with a violent storm of wind, and flashes of the strongest and most vivid lightning and heavy thunder, which is followed by rain. These storms sometimes last for half an hour or more; and when they disperse they leave the air greatly freshened, and the sky of a deep, clear, and transparent blue. When they occur near the full moon, the whole atmosphere is illuminated by a soft but brilliant silver light, attended with gentle airs, as Shakespeare has expressed—

"When the sweet wind did gently kiss the trees,
"And they did make no noise."

Passing by the city of Moorshedabad, on the evening of a Mussulman holiday, I was much entertained to see the river covered with innumerable lights, just floating above the surface of the water. Such an uncommon appearance was, at first, difficult to account for; but I found, upon enquiry, that upon these occasions they fabricate a number of small lamps, which they light and set afloat on the river: the stream constantly running down, they are carried to a confiderable diftance, and laft for many hours. After a paffage of a few days from Mongheir, I arrived at Calcutta. Several of the fubjects I had collected in my journey were painted for the Honourable the then Governor General; two of them on a large fcale, viz. the Falls of Mootejerna, and the Ruins of Rajemahel.

CHAP. III.

Embark in the Train of the Governor General—Boats of the Country defcribed—Remarks on thofe of the South Sea— Views on the River—Dutch, French, and Danifh Settlements—Sir Eyre Coote's—Coffimbuzen—Sir John D'Oyley's —Patna—Reception of the Governor there—Mofque of Moonhier—Arrive at Buxar—Gazipoor—Curious Ruins— Benares—Arreft of the Rajah—Infurrection at Benares— Principal Events of the War—Flight from Benares, and Return thither.

I DID not remain long in the capital of Bengal, on my return from Mongheir, before a new opportunity was prefented to me of again indulging the curiofity which I felt both as an artift and a man, to enlarge my acquaintance with a country fo fertile in the beauties of nature at leaft. It being determined by the Bengal Government that it was expedient, for the public utility, that the Governor General fhould make a tour through a part of the country, Mr. Haftings, with that liberality and attention to the arts which has ever characterized his conduct, acceded to my requeft, and permitted me to accompany him.

ON the 25th of June, 1781, therefore, I embarked in a budgerow for this expedition. The periodical rains had now commenced, and every natural object prefented a new face, with fuch a frefhnefs of verdure, and with fuch vigour and fulnefs of foliage, that all nature appeared in the utmoſt luxuriance. From the number of gentlemen who neceffarily attended the Governor General, the fleet was very large, and confiſted of every variety of the boats of the country, except thofe which are called burs, and of which we met with feveral in our courfe. Thefe veffels are large rude barks, the fides of which are raifed very high, and fewed together with the fibres of the cocoa nut tree. They have only a fingle maſt, with a large fquare fail, and the bottoms of them are nearly flat. They take in a great quantity of water from their fides and bottoms, which compels the crew to employ fome people continually in bailing. They are ufed for the carriage of cotton, and other very bulky materials, the weight of which cannot bear any proportion to their fize. Indeed, it would be impracticable to employ boats which were calculated to draw any confiderable quantity of water on this river, as the navigation is extremely dangerous, from the fands being conſtantly fhifting. I have known an ifland, four miles in length, and containing fome villages, wholly fwept away in one feafon; in the mean time, at a little diſtance, other iſlands were formed, from the fands being thrown up. This phenomenon took place off the point of Rajemahel, in the year 1782.

INDIA. 39

THE boats used by the natives for travelling, and also by Europeans, are the budgerows, which both sail and row: they have in general from twelve to twenty oars. These boats vary in their size according to the condition of their owners; some may be about sixty feet in length, having very high sterns; many of them twelve feet from the water's edge, and quite sharp at the upper point; in the center they are broad, having a considerable bearing in the water, and quite sharp forward. They are steered with a large paddle or oar, extending ten feet from the stern; and there is generally one mast in the center, on which is hoisted a large square sail: they have likewise a topmast, on which is a square sail for fine weather. These boats are ill calculated to go near the wind, and indeed are dangerous, from the great weight abaft; they are, however, extremely commodious, having in the center a small verander, or open portico, opening by a door into a handsome room, lighted by a range of windows on each side. This is the dining or sitting room, within which is a convenient bed chamber, generally containing a small closet: the heighth of the sitting room is usually from seven to nine feet. Besides this boat, a gentleman is usually attended by two others; a pulwah, for the accommodation of the kitchen, and a smaller boat, a paunchway, which is destined to convey him either on shore or on board, as it frequently happens that the budgerow cannot come close to the shores, where he might wish to land. These boats sail more expeditiously than the budgerows; but the paunchways are nearly of the fame general conſtruction, with this difference, that the greateſt breadth is ſomewhat farther aft, and the ſterns lower: the pulwahs are a broad boat, and not ſo ſharp forward or aft as the other two. The Engliſh gentlemen have made great improvements on the budgerow in Bengal, by introducing a broad flat floor, ſquare ſterns, and broad bows. Theſe boats are much ſafer, ſail near and keep their wind, and there is no danger attending their taking the ground; they are, beſides, calculated for carrying a greater quantity of ſail. Another boat of this country, which is very curiouſly conſtructed, is called a Moor-punky: theſe are very long and narrow, ſometimes extending to upwards of an hundred feet in length, and not more than eight feet in breadth; they are always paddled, ſometimes by forty men, and are ſteered by a large paddle from the ſtern, which riſes either in the ſhape of a peacock, a ſnake, or ſome other animal. The perſons employed to paddle are directed by a man who ſtands up, and ſometimes he makes uſe of a branch of a plant to direct their motions. In one part of the ſtern is a canopy ſupported by pillars, in which are ſeated the owner and his friends, who partake together of the refreſhing breezes of the evening. Theſe boats are very expenſive, owing to the beautiful decorations of painted and gilt ornaments, which are highly varniſhed, and exhibit a very conſiderable degree of taſte. It was curious to me to obſerve the perfect ſimilarity in manners between the inhabitants of this country and the people of Otaheite in theſe water excurfions. The pleafure boats of the South Sea iflanders are, in many inftances, fimilar to thefe: working in an ocean, they found the neceffity of applying an out rigger, or of lafhing two veffels together, to prevent overfetting. Like the boats I am fpeaking of, they are worked by paddles, and are alfo directed by a man holding a branch, who, in common with the perfon in the Moor-punky, ufes much gefticulation, and tells his ftory to excite either laughter or exertion. My former paffage down the river to Calcutta was too rapid to allow of more obfervation than what related to the general appearance of the villages and towns on its banks. The ftream is ufually calculated to run at the rate of five miles an hour; but the rapidity of the flood, during the rainy feafon, is increafed, and round fome of the points in the river it is very great. Should it be calm weather when the flood is thus impetuous, the boatmen endure much fatigue in towing round thefe points againft the ftream, and particularly fo where the banks are very high; and fome of them, in the great river, are equal to the top of the maft of a common budgerow.

AT a fmall diftance above Calcutta is the Danifh fettlement of Serampoor, where there is a neat town, which carries on a confiderable trade. Both fides of the river are decorated with a few houfes belonging to Englifh gentlemen: at Ghiretty, twenty miles from Calcutta, is a very fine feat, which, in the year 1781, was inhabited by the family of the late Sir Eyre Coote, who at that time was fighting the battles of his country on the plains of the Carnatic; where his health and life fell a sacrifice to his great exertions. With an army of never more than seven thousand effective men, this experienced General kept the whole power of Hyder Ally at bay, and at all times was superior in action to the multitudes of the enemy, who were supported by a most formidable train of artillery, and immense bodies of cavalry.

A LITTLE above this is the French settlement of Chandernagore, and the ruins of the fort evince it to have been considerable. The fort was destroyed by Commodore Watson in 1758, in a severe action, which was particularly distinguished by the gallantry of Captain Speke, who lost his son on the quarter-deck of his own ship during the engagement. Near to this is the town of Chinsurah, the Dutch settlement, on the banks of the river: this town is very distinguishable at a considerable distance, and has a handsome appearance. It contains several good houses, and a church, with a little mole projecting into the river. Chinsurah lies nearly midway between Chandernagore and the old town of Hoogly, which is now nearly in ruins, but possesses many vestiges of its former greatness. In the beginning of this century it was the great mart for the export trade of Bengal to Europe. From this place we pass by Culna and Nuddea, (both considerable towns) in our way to Cutwa, which was made famous by the retreat of Aliverdy Cawn, in the face of a large Marhatta army, in May 1742. After paffing Plaffy, which has been already mentioned, is the great military ftation, in Bengal, Burhampoor, where there are barracks for ten thoufand men; and a little above is the ifland of Coffimbuzar, in which is a factory belonging to the Englifh company, where a commercial refident is conftantly ftationed: the gentleman then refident was Mr. S. Droz, whofe polite attentions to me I fhall always remember with pleafure. On this ifland there is likewife a Dutch factory. At a fhort diftance from Coffimbuzar is the city of Moorfhedabad, where, at the period of which I am fpeaking, refided Sir John D'Oyley, then engaged in a political department. The liberality and attentions of this gentleman to every perfon travelling this road are well known; and in his houfe, I may truly fay, reigned the very fpirit of old Englifh hofpitality. From Moorfhedabad the Hoogly river continues to Sooty, where is the entrance into the Ganges. From this place to Mongheir it is ufual to keep on the weftern fhore, and nearly all the way to Patna, unlefs a leading breeze from the fouthward and eaftward fhould enable the boatmen to fteer as nearly from point to point as the fhoals will admit. Every where on either fide of the river there are collections of villages, and the country is in high cultivation.

WHEN the fleet arrived at the city of Patna the fhores were lined with people, the windows in the houfes on the banks of the river were filled, even the tops of the buildings and every wall was crouded, fo that when the Governor General went on fhore, it was fcarcely poffible to proceed, from the multitude, which preffed on every fide, to falute him. When he had paffed them, all appeared ftruck with the fimplicity of his appearance, and his ready and conftant attention to prevent any injury to the meaneft individual from the irrafcibility of his Chubdars, or other fervants, who endeavoured to keep them from preffing in. They could not but contraft this appearance and conduct with that of their Nabobs, whom they had never feen except mounted on lofty elephants, and glittering in fplendor with their train, followed by the foldiery to keep off the multitude from offending their arrogance and pride.

The city of Patna, the principal feat of the province and government of Bahar, is long and narrow, containing a great number of inhabitants: this is the refidence of the political and commercial chiefs, and the courts of juftice of the province. It has been famous for ages. Major Rennel, whofe judgement is fcarcely to be difputed, places the ancient city of Palebothra upon the fcite of Patna. The buildings are high, and the ftreets narrow and far from clean. Patna contains a fort, in which were confined the prifoners taken by Meer Coffim, Nabob of Bengal, in the war of 1764, by whofe order they were maffacred. The execution of this moft atrocious act was committed to Summaroo, a French renegado in the fervice of the Nabob. The confequence of this fcene of horror was, the expulfion of the Nabob, who afterwards drew the late Sujah ul Dowlah, Nabob of Oude, into a war with the Englifh, which terminated fo favourably and fo honourably to the Britifh character at the battle of Buxar; when a peace was made, leaving the conquerors in the undifturbed poffeffion of Bengal, Bahar, and part of Orixa. Meer Coffim became afterwards, from his crimes, an outcaft from fociety, and is reported to have died of want under the walls of Delhi, being prohibited from entering the city.

From Patna I made an excurfion inland, about five cofs, to view the mofque of Moonhier, on the river Soane. This building, though not large, is certainly very beautiful: it is a fquare, with pavilions rifing from the angles; and in the center is a majeftic dome, the top of which is finifhed by what the Indian architects call a cullus: the line of the curve of the dome is not broken, but is continued by an inverted curve until it finifhes in a crefcent. I cannot but greatly prefer this to the manner in which all great domes are finifhed in Europe, by erecting a fmall building on the top, which, at the point of contact with the dome, has a fharp angle. The outer furface of this dome is ornamented by plantane leaves cut in ftone, covering the whole; the lines interfect each other in great lozenges, and form altogether a beautiful ornament. The great entrance to the mofque is similar to many of the doors to our large Gothic cathedrals, having columns diminishing as it were in perspective to the inner door. There is a large tank belonging to it, with several buildings rising from the water, containing pavilions. The whole, however, is much decayed.

THE river Soane falls into the Ganges a little above Patna: at a small distance from Patna is Bankepour, where are the residences of the English gentlemen, and near to which is the military station of Dinapour.

FROM Patna I followed the fleet, and passed the mouth of the river Caramnassa, the boundary of Bahar, and on the 12th of August arrived at Buxar. This is a fort and small military station, and was, at the time I was there, commanded by Major Eaton. We proceeded from this place to Gazipoor, on the eastern shore of the Ganges. At this place are the ruins of a fine palace, built in the beginning of this century. It is raised on a high bank, and on a point commanding two great reaches of the river, up and down. From the bank, which is full thirty feet from the water, is raised another basement of brick and masonry fifteen feet high, in which are some apartments: on this is the building, which is an oblong square, with great pavilions at the angles, and in the center of each side: the whole is an open space, supported by colonades surrounding it. Within, on the floor of the building, is a channel for water about four feet wide; it encircles the floor, and, at equal fpaces, there were formerly fountains. In the center of the building is a fpace fufficient to contain twenty people.

NEARLY adjoining to this palace is a building for the purpofe of raifing water for the fountains, and fupplying them by the means of pipes, which communicate with each other.

ABOUT two miles inland from the river are the remains of a ferai; and, nearly adjoining, tombs, built at the fame period as the palace. Thefe buildings are in a fine tafte of Moorifh architecture, and in very good repair. Views of both the palace and tombs are exhibited to the public in a work which I publifhed, containing Views in India.

FROM Gazipoor I proceeded to Benares, a diftance of twenty Englifh miles, and arrived there the day after the Governor General with his fuite.

I FELT a real pleafure on my arrival at this place, from being able to contemplate the pure Hindoo manners, arts, buildings, and cuftoms, undepraved by any intermixture with the Mahomedans; and laid my plans for obferving with the utmoft attention whatever came within the fphere of a painter's notice. The unhappy events that immediately fucceeded fruftrated, for the prefent, thofe defigns.

It would give me pleasure to satisfy the curiosity of the reader concerning the circumstances of that war, but it would be foreign to the object of these pages to enter upon a minute detail; and the public is already in possession of the great outline of the facts. Some notes, however, which I made on the spot, and at the time, may prove not quite uninteresting, and I flatter myself will contain something of original information.

It is not my business to enter into the question respecting the rights of the government in different countries and those of the governed. Facts are my object, and such alone as fell within the limited and confined sphere of my notice. On my arrival, the 15th of August, the general conversation turned upon the conduct of Cheyt Sing, the Zemendar of the province. It is necessary in this place to remark, that the word Zemendar implies simply a land-holder, either by a right of inheritance, or as a renter merely; if by right of inheritance, the government, virtually being the proprietors of the soil, if they think proper may possess themselves of it by the laws of Hindostan, paying to the Zemendar ten per cent. out of such Zemendary. Rajah Cheyt Sing had met the Governor General at Buxar, attended with a considerable train, and a large fleet of boats, in which were two thousand armed men, selected from the flower of the military of Benares, and supposed at the time, and reasonably so, to be intended for the purpose of supporting him in the refufal of fuch demands as might be made upon him by the Governor General, and to prevent the exertion of force in fupport of the Britifh authority.

THE caufe of difagreement between the Britifh government and the Zemendar of Benares is well known. It is, however, merely an act of common juftice to ftate, that, during my whole refidence in India, I never fo much as heard the guilt and perfidy of Cheyt Sing once called in queftion. It was notorious that he was in the intereft of the enemy; and it was equally notorious that he with-held, under the moft trifling and falfe pretences, the affiftance which was demanded of him, and which by the nature of his treaty he was bound to furnifh: in a word, it was notorious to every perfon that he wanted only a convenient opportunity to withdraw his allegiance from the company.

AFTER feveral letters and meffages had paffed between Cheyt Sing and the Governor General, the Refident, Mr. Markham, received orders to put the Rajah under arreft, at his houfe at Sewalla Gaut, on the banks of the river, to which he quietly fubmitted, without any appearance of oppofition. This was on the 16th; and about one o'clock in the afternoon we were informed that a large body of the Rajah's people had croffed from Ramnagur to the Benares fide of the river, and had furrounded the Rajah's houfe. A note was at the fame time received by the Refident, Mr.

Markham, from Lieutenant Staulker, who had been left with two companies of Major Popham's grenadier seapoys as a guard, saying that the people began to be troublesome, and requesting an immediate supply of ammunition. It was now found that such delicacy had been observed towards the Rajah, in order to prevent any suspicion being entertained of an intention to carry the punishment farther than was really proposed, that the seapoys muskets were not loaded, nor had they (as no serious opposition was expected) any ammunition. To this unfortunate circumstance may be attributed the unhappy fate of three very gallant officers, Lieutenants Staulker, Scott, and Sims, and two compleat companies of grenadier seapoys, not more than twenty escaping with their lives, and numbers of those miserably wounded.

As soon as the disturbance became known, Major Popham, who was then at Benares, set off immediately for his camp at Marwaddy, about two cofs (or four miles) from the town, to lead the remainder of his people to the assistance of their fellow soldiers. His utmost exertions enabled them to arrive only in sufficient time to be the melancholy spectators of this horrid slaughter, without the power of revenging it, as the rebels had dispersed, and the Rajah had found means to make his escape.

FORTUNATELY for the English party in Benares, the rebels were satisfied with what they had effected, the liberation of the Rajah and the maſſacre of the ſeapoys ; but had they attacked the Governor General in his then defenceleſs ſituation, every perſon with him muſt have fallen a ſacrifice to their fury.

THE following day every Engliſhman attended the funeral of Lieutenants Staulker, Scott, and Sims; and ſome time after a monument to their memory was raiſed over their remains. The gloom that ſucceeded was truly melancholy; the buſineſs of the city was ſtopt, and it was deſerted by great numbers of the inhabitants. In paſſing through the ſtreets knots of people, all of them armed, were obſerved ſecretly conſulting. From this ſituation we were rouſed by an unhappy affair, ariſing from the ill-judged ambition of Captain Mayaffer, who commanded the remainder of Major Popham's detachment at Mizapoor, on the oppoſite ſide of the river, conſiſting of a battalion of ſeapoys, and Captain Doxat's corps of chaſſeurs, reinforced by Captain Blair's battalion of ſeapoys from Chunar. This officer, contrary to poſitive orders, led the troops to the attack of Ramnagur, a fort and town on the oppoſite ſide of the river to Benares. The ſtreets of this town are narrow, and every houſe being built with ſtone, they became each a fortification, which was filled with the Rajah's people. The conſequence of this raſh conduct was, the loſs of Captain Mayaffer, Captain Doxat, thirty-three of the corps of chaſſeurs, two guns, one howitzer, and one hundred and three men of all denominations. The news of this check reached us on the 21ſt. in the morning, and was ſoon followed by advices of the intentions of the rebels to make an attack on Benares that night; it was therefore thought adviſable to leave this place of inſecurity for Chunar, a diſtance of twenty miles. This reſolution was taken at ſeven in the evening, and the whole party was clear of the town by half paſt eight o'clock. The confuſion natural on ſuch an occaſion ſoon ſubſided; and the party, including ſervants, &c. with the troops, which amounted to about four hundred men, ſafely arrived oppoſite Chunar in the morning at ſeven o'clock. The night fortunately turned out the moſt favourable poſſible; it was light, clear, and cool. As the reſolution was ſuddenly taken, I was under the neceſſity of leaving behind me the whole of my baggage, excepting my drawings, and a few changes of linen, which I had thrown into my pallankeen, and which in the confuſion of the night I loſt ſight of, but found my ſervants on the following day. In the party was Beneram Pundit, the Berar Vakeel,* and his brother Biſſumber Pundit, who, from motives of the ſtrongeſt perſonal attachment to Mr. Haſtings, left their family in Benares, to attend him, and ſet what in that country is a very extraordinary example, a native voluntarily ſharing in the dangers and diſtreſſes of a European, without a view to his own private advantage.

* Vakeel is an Agent from one court to another.

INDIA. 53

ON this occafion it cannot be improper to mention the handfome and liberal conduct of every gentleman in the garrifon of Chunar to thofe who attended the Governor General. I feel ftrongly the attentions fhewn me at this time by my friend Major, now Colonel Gardner, at whofe houfe, during my ftay at Chunar, I received every kind of hofpitality.

THE war was now completely commenced, with great difadvantage on the part of the Englifh; their number fmall, and befieged in a fort, without provifion to laft a month, or money to pay the few troops, which were already confiderably in arrears, owing to the mifconduct of the Rajah, who had now fixed his ftandard on the fort of Lutteefpoor, in the jungles,* and who was recruiting his army. The feveral orders that had been fent by the Governor General to the commanding officers, who were within a moderate diftance, to march to his affiftance, were either cut off by the enemy, or, from the fears of the meffengers, thefe orders were fecreted, and were never heard of afterwards. One of the Hircarrahs,† however, reached Lieutenant Polhil, then at Allahabad, who immediately marched with his corps of three hundred and eighty men, and reached the oppofite fhore of Chunar on the 27th. In the mean time, a perfon in the fervice of

* Jungles, clofe woods.

† Hircarrahs are fervants, ufed for carrying orders or meffages to any diftance.

Cheyt Sing, at Iionpoor, on the river Goomty, had collected a body of two thousand matchlock men, and one hundred and fifty horse, and had taken post at a small fort called Seker, on the opposite side of the river to Chunar. This man Lieutenant Polhil received orders to attack on the following morning, which order he executed with success: he drove the enemy, and took possession of the fort, and secured a considerable quantity of grain. This was a valuable acquisition to the party, for it was now found, from the temper of the people and the complexion of the times, that scarcely as much grain could be procured as would serve the daily consumption of the garrison. The Rajah's force at this time was said to be ten thousand strong, and his ostensible force was daily increasing.

MAJOR Popham's camp lay at two miles distance from the fort; and on the third of September he detached a party, under the command of Captain Blair, with an intention to break up a camp of the enemy which was formed under the walls of Pateeta, and which was carried into execution with great gallantry, though with considerable loss. Pateeta is a large town, surrounded by a rampart, and defended by a fort.

THE news of the insurrection had spread to a considerable distance, and a force was detached from Cawnpoor, and from Lucknow, to the assistance of the Governor General, under Majors Crab and Roberts, the firſt of which reached Chunar on the 10th of September, and the latter gentleman on the 13th. Effective meaſures were then taken to put a final period to the war, by attacking vigorouſly both the fort of Pateeta and that of Lutteefpoor, and both attacks happily ſucceeded on the ſame day, the Rajah flying from Lutteefpoor to take ſanctuary in his ſtrong hold of Bidjegur. I ſhould have remarked, that Pateeta lies about four miles north of Chunar, and Lutteefpoor ten miles beyond, in the ſame direction: Bidjegur is fifty miles from Chunar.

THE cruel and ſanguinary difpoſition of Cheyt Sing was manifeſted, during his reſidence in Lutteefpoor, by an action of peculiar atrocity. Some wounded men who were taken priſoners in the camp that was left at Mirzapoor, on the retreat of the troops after the unhappy affair of Captain Mayaffer, had been conveyed to Lutteefpoor, where they were detained as priſoners. Upon hearing of the ſuccefs of Captain Blair's party, the Rajah ordered the unhappy men to be bound and carried into the woods, and to be there maſſacred in cold blood. One poor creature only eſcaped in a very mangled condition into Chunar.

THE fort of Chunar is ſituated on the Ganges, near twenty miles above the city of Benares: it is built on a rock, which is fortified all round by a wall, and towers at various diſtances. At that end overlooking the river is ſituated the citadel, which has formerly been ſtrong. This fort is ſaid to be of the higheſt antiquity, and originally built by the Hindoos. In the citadel there is an altar, conſiſting of a plain black marble ſlab, on which the tutelary deity of the place is traditionally at all times ſuppoſed to be ſeated, except from ſun-riſe until nine o'clock in the morning, when he is at Benares, during which time, from the ſuperſtition of the Hindoos, attacks may be made with a proſpect of ſucceſs. In various parts of the fort there are old ſculptures of the Hindoo divinities, now nearly defaced by time. There are likewiſe on the gates ſome old Perſian inſcriptions, mentioning in whoſe reign, and by whom, the fort was repaired and ſtrengthened.

This has always been conſidered as a poſt of great conſequence upon the Ganges, from its inſulated ſituation, projecting forwards to a conſiderable extent, and being of conſiderable heighth. It was beſieged by the Engliſh in the war carried on, during the years 1764 and 1765, againſt the late Nabob Sujah ul Dowlah when he joined Meer Coſſim, and was gallantly defended by its commandant, an Abyſſinian in the ſervice of that prince.

The firſt attempt of the Engliſh againſt Chunar was unſucceſsful; but afterwards, on the fall of Allahabad, the commandant finding that the whole country had ſubmitted to the Engliſh, and that his maſter's affairs were deſperate, thought it needlefs to hold out any longer, and on the 7th of February, 1765, he furrendered the Fort to Major, now General Stibbert; it was afterwards reftored to the Nabob, when the peace was fettled with that Prince; and in 1772, it was formally ceded by him to the Englifh Eaft India Company, in exchange for the Fort of Allahabad. At this place is kept the magazine of ammunition and artillery for the Brigade at Cawnpore.

DURING my ftay at Chunar I made feveral drawings of the Fort, and one of Pateeta. As the war was, however, now concluded, except obtaining poffeffion of Bidjegur (to which place Major Popham proceeded with his whole force), the whole party returned with the Governor General, through Ramnagur, to Benares, and arrived there the 28th of September; after which I had fufficient leifure and opportunity for my particular and profeffional purfuits.

CHAP. IV.

Defcription of Benares—Elegant Fafcade—Hindoo Temples—Differtation on the Hindoo, Moorifh, and Gothic Architecture.

THE city of Benares being the capital of a large diftrict, and particularly marked as the feat of the Bramin learning, it cannot but be confidered as an object of particular curiofity, more efpecially, fince the fame manners and cuftoms prevail amongft thefe people at this day, as at the remoteft period that can be traced in hiftory: and in no inftances of religious or civil life have they admitted of any innovations from foreigners. According to univerfal report, this is one of the moft ancient Hindoo cities; and if the accounts of their own antiquity may be depended upon, it is, perhaps, the oldeft in the world. Major Rennell, however, entertains a different opinion on this fubject, from its not being mentioned by the Syrian Embaffadors foon after the time of Alexander, and from its being unnoticed by Pliny; and I have too great a deference for fuch an authority, to be at all inclined to difpute it, whatever may be the claims to antiquity which are preferred in favour of this city.

IT certainly is curious, and highly entertaining to an inquifitive mind, to affociate with a people whofe manners are more than three thousand years old; and to observe in them that attention and polished behaviour which usually marks the most highly civilized state of society.

The distance of Benares from Calcutta, by the nearest road, according to Major Rennell, is 460 miles; by water, that distance is greatly increased. This city anciently bore the name of Kasi, but at what period it received its present name the page of history is silent. It is built on the north side of the river, which is here very broad, and the banks of which are very high: from the water, its appearance is extremely beautiful; the great variety of the buildings strikes the eye, and the whole view is much improved by innumerable flights of stone steps, which are either entrances into the several temples, or to the houses. Several Hindoo temples greatly embellish the banks of the river, and are all ascended to by Gauts, or flights of steps, such as I have already noticed. Many other public and private buildings possess also considerable magnificence. Several of these I have painted, and some on a large scale, such as I conceived the subjects demanded. Many buildings on the banks of the river, which engage the attention, and invite to further observation, prove, on a more minute investigation, to be only embankments, to prevent the overflowing of the water from carrying away the banks at the season of the periodical rains, and for some time after, when the river is high, and the current strong. The most considerable of thefe embankments is called Gelfi Gaut; the fplendor and elegance of which, as a building, I was induced to examine, but found, upon afcending the large flight of fteps from the river, nothing behind this beautiful fafcade but the natural bank, and on the top a planted garden. In the centre of the building, over the river, is a kind of turret, raifed and covered, for the purpofe of enjoying the frefhnefs of the evening air; and, at the extreme angles, two pavilions crowned with domes, which have the fame deftination. Moft of thefe buildings have been erected by the charitable contributions of the wealthy, for the benefit of the public.

NEARLY in the centre of the city is a confiderable Mahomedan mofque, with two minarets: the height from the water to the top of the minarets is 232 feet. This building was raifed by that moft intolerant and ambitious of human beings, the Emperor Aurungzebe, who deftroyed a magnificent temple of the Hindoos on this fpot, and built the prefent mofque, of the fame extent and height as the building he deftroyed.

THE ftreets in the city are narrow, and not kept in fuch good order as I expected, from fome Hindoo villages I had before feen. The houfes are very high; I obferved fome in which I counted five ftories, each inhabited by different families. The more wealthy Hindoos, however, live in detached houfes, with open courts, furrounded by a wall. The heat, in this place, is confidered as very great in the hot months, not only from its natural fituation, but from the houfes being all built of free ftone, as well as from the narrownefs of the ftreets, which produce double and treble reflections of the fun's rays: from the month of March, therefore, to the ufual fetting in of the rains in the latter end of June, its heat muft be intolerable.

SURROUNDING the city are many ruins of buildings, the effects of Mahomedan intolerance. One is a large circular edifice, having evidently been a Hindoo temple, or part of one; there are ftill veftiges of fome of the ornaments; and on one part I found the Grecian fcroll.

DURING my ftudies at Benares, when I was making drawings of fome Bramins, and feveral other perfons who were entering and departing from a temple named Vifs Visfha, my attention was called to the building itfelf, and the more I regarded it, the more I was furprized to difcover ornaments upon it which were familiar to my eyes. I then determined to make a fketch of the whole, which I executed, as well as a more complete drawing of one of the columns; for on accurately obferving the building in all its parts, I found each column to contain the different ornaments which were found in the other parts of the building.

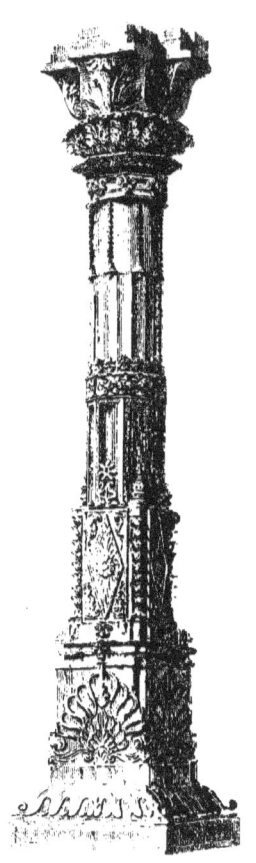

INDIA. 63

For the fatisfaction of my readers a very careful engraving is annexed, which was executed from the drawing made upon the fpot.

It is certainly curious to obferve moft of the ornamental parts of Grecian architecture appearing in a building erected on the plains of Hindoftan. I was indeed much ftruck with this circumftance, and led to reflect upon it fo frequently, that I was at length tempted to commit to paper a few thoughts on thefe different ftyles of architecture, which, in the form of a pamphlet upon the fubject, was accompanied by two large plates engraved from pictures, entitled, *Views of the Gate leading to the Tomb of Acbar at Secundii, and the Maufoleum of the Emperor Shere Shah at Safferam*. As the effay accompanying thefe plates was printed on a fcale equal to the plates, and as I have fince found that it could not on that account be read with any convenience, I determined to introduce the fubftance of it in this place, as being immediately connected with the fubject which is now before us, and I conceive perfectly calculated for a work profeffedly dedicated, in fome meafure, to the hiftory and progrefs of the arts in India.

As I am neither fufficiently qualified, nor willing to lofe myfelf in the unfathomable, and perhaps impenetrable darknefs of Eaftern antiquities, I fhall not, for the prefent, fay any thing on the characteriftic difference of the original Hindoo, and the more modern ftyle of Moorifh Architecture, in which all the great monuments are constructed; but I shall confine myself to a few loose remarks on the prototypes, or first models of architecture, as far as it is an art both of taste and convenience.

That the Grecian Architecture comprizes all that is excellent in the art, I cannot help considering as a doctrine, which is in itself as erroneous and servile, as in its consequences it is destructive of every hope of improvement. Architecture undoubtedly should, and must be adapted, to all the climates and countries which mankind inhabit, and is variously, more than any other art, influenced and modified by the nature of the climate and materials, as well as by the habits and pursuits of the inhabitants.

I have not read Father Ladola's famous dissertation on the absurdity of the misplaced and unprincipled imitation of Greek architecture; nor am I in the least prejudiced against its very eminent beauties and perfections: but why should we admire it in an exclusive manner; or, blind to the majesty, boldness, and magnificence of the Egyptian, Hindoo, Moorish, and Gothic, as admirable wonders of architecture, unmercifully blame and despise them, because they are more various in their forms, and not reducible to the precise rules of the Greek hut, prototype, and column? or because in smaller parts, perhaps accidentally similar, their proportions are different from those to which we are become familiar by habit.

ALLOWING what muſt be allowed, that the Greek columns, as they are drawn and applied by genius, are the moſt beautiful ſtone repreſentations of the wooden props or ſupports of their original hut, and that in their general forms, and each ſubordinate part, they are the *ne plus ultra* of ſimplicity, ſtrength, and elegance, ſhall we precipitately determine, that the whole excellence of architecture depends on the column alone, or forget that its great effect depends rather upon the great maſſes and forms, and upon the ſymmetry, ſtrength, and conveniency?

HOWEVER partial I muſt feel, from habit and education, to the Greeks, whoſe free and unfettered genius, in a long ſeries of ages, improved the original hut of a woody country into the incomparable beauties of a marble temple or palace; yet I freely avow that this by no means prevents my entertaining a ſimilar partiality for countries, where different models have been brought to an equal perfection. The forms of the firſt habitations have differed, as the reſpective countries, climates, and manners of the builders, and as the nature, abundance, or ſcantineſs of materials have directed.

CAVERNS, deep vallies, ſhaggy over-hanging rocks, hollow trees, and the thick impenetrable foliage of the foreſt, have been equally the natural retreat and occaſional habitation of the wild beaſts, and of men whom different accidents have left unacquainted with the comforts of ſociety, expoſed to the inclemencies of the seasons, or to the apprehension of dangers from animals of prey, or the no less dangerous enemies of their own species. Men are neither born with tools to build with, nor can be supposed to have intuitively an innate idea of any particular form of habitation, such as bountiful nature has assigned to the beaver, the swallow, or the bee; but man is born with a native sense of his wants, and with judgment and intellectual powers to improve his situation by such means, as the country affords, and as the climate will suggest.

Thus far I can venture to state, not only from what I have read, but likewise by a stronger conviction, from what I have seen in the various climates and parts of the world in which I have beheld mankind, in almost every stage of negative or positive civilization.

The hollow tree, and the thick foliage of the forest, into which even Kings of Ithaca and Britain have retired, are fitter for occasional than for permanent residence. They appear evidently imitated in the wigwams of the torpid, wretched, unsettled Pecherais on the frozen coast of Terra del Fuego; of the equally independent, but not more fortunate New Hollanders, in a milder climate; and of the more civilized and sagacious hunting savages of North America.

These wigwams, nearly the same every where as to form, differ in various countries only in the nature of the materials they are built with, such as the boughs of trees, shrubs, creeping plants, reeds, sods, and grass. Now, if any of these wandering families of hunters and fishermen should become stationary, or form into larger societies, they would soon be disposed to give to their habitations as much durability and conveniency as their climates, materials, and manner of life would admit of; nor is it probable they would lose sight of their prototype, the wigwam, or materially deviate from it in the external form of their more capacious erection. For constant residence, these would be improved into the various thatches and huts which I have seen in the South Sea Islands, and which the Negroes on the Coast of Guinea, and the Hottentots, inhabit; high and low, circular or square, open at all sides, inclosed with palisades, matting, or wicker-work hurdles, lattice, or mud walls. They will raise them on piles above the ground, and, as it were, suspend them in the air, in countries where the dampness of the soil, or sudden inundations, would endanger their lives and property; as on the banks of the Marannon, or Oroonoko, in Guiana, and in the inland parts of Surinam: they will keep them low, and, as it were, sink them under ground, in cold climates, where heavy blasts of wind and snow teach them such methods of self-defence. Wandering nations, of herdsmen, fishermen, and warriors, such as the Arabs, Calmucks, Monguls, Tonquesees, Tartars, Esquimeaux, Greenlanders, Laplanders, Samojedes, and Ostiacks, find in the skins of their cattle, of their flocks, and of their fishes, materials; and in their camels, horses, bullocks, and fishing boats, conveyances of portable huts, and imitations of their original wigwams, huts and tents, which in shape will differ more or less, according to the different materials they are made of. We find them of seal and rein deer skins in the north, of hides, felt, or matting; in Arabia or Tartary, in the form of cones, with square roofs, and open or shut at the sides.

THE different habitations will retain more or less of their primitive form in proportion as the different builders remain independent and unmixed, unconnected, and in the same state and culture; and as habit reconciles the human mind to almost every thing, each of these nations or tribes will regard their primitive habitations with the same eye of partiality as they are prejudiced in favour of their respective countries; but when encreasing opulence, ambition, or succesful oppression, create artificial wants, and the great look for more convenience and distinction, the national primitive hut or tent will be enlarged, and embellished with what is costly among them. When emigrations to foreign countries take place, their prototype will follow the colonist, and genius will at last stretch and improve it to the last degree of perfection of which it is capable. What this is, or may be, in architecture, we see with admiration exemplified in the old Greek and Roman architecture, which is the thatched wooden hut, metamorphofed by genius into a marble edifice, and yet expreffing its original parts in fuch proportions as are confiftent with the nature of ftone and marble. Agreeably to the fame principle, the moft elegant Chinefe buildings are evidently imitations of the tent made of bamboo, where ftrength and flender tapering form admit of higher proportions and wider intercolumniations, and muft, of courfe, make the Greek marble column and its narrow intercolumniation appear heavy in comparifon with the Chinefe. The Chinefe idea of the beauties of their architecture muft differ from that of the Greeks, and the Greek rule of architectural beauty cannot reafonably be applied to the principle and materials of Chinefe buildings. How far all the above prototypes of buildings are improveable, muft be left to the future exertions of genius.

THE oblong and tapering huts of the people of Eafter Ifland in the Southern Ocean, are hardly improveable in that country, which is almoft deftitute of timber. An active people, fuch as its former inhabitants feem to have been, might, indeed, imitate them in ftone; but would thefe huts fuggeft any idea but that of ribbed oblong arches, tapering on every fide? Even the fimple wigwam will, under the influence of fortunate circumftances, be adorned by genius with all the pomp of Flora; the rofe, the vine, the honey-fuckle, and the gourd, will be entwined; they will be formed into cool and fhady bowers, like thofe which the glowing imagination of Milton affigned to our firft parents in the Garden of Eden.

THE cavern and grotto, by nature fitted for the fafe retreat and habitation of man, has in itfelf many advantages; in particular, a folidity and durability, which art has never been able fuccefsfully to imitate: its impenetrable fides and external form are the mountain itfelf.

WHEN airy, fpacious, and lofty within, on a rifing ground, commanding an extenfive profpect and a fpring, on the banks of rivers, or in the cliffs on the fea fhore, how defirable in a burning climate; impenetrable to wind and weather, how acceptable in cold climates, which are deprived of timber. Let us have a nearer view of its gloomy receffes.

THEY are indifcriminately found in every climate; but in mountainous countries only, in which, as the Swifs philofophers tell us, with a particular complacency to themfelves, fagacity fooner ripens into genius, and in which the materials for building artificial mountains and caves are obvious at every ftep. Violence and fuperior force would foon take poffeffion of thofe which are fitteft for habitation and fafety. The bones and remains of the largeft and ficrceft wild beafts, fuch as the elephant, rhinoceros, lion, tiger, bear, and wolf, formerly the lords of the wildernefs, are ftill found in many of them, and conftitute fo many proofs of their exclufive poffeffion. Is it to be wondered at, that the ftouteft, fierceft, and craftieft, amongft the lords of the whole creation, fhould alfo have laid hold and kept fimilar poffeffion of them from the remoteft antiquity?

INDIA.

A GOOD cavern was then a superb palace; under certain circumstances it is so still. If these great men, or usurpers, became afterwards objects of superstitious adoration, or if they have themselves been the framers of any system of superstition, then we shall no longer be at a loss to account for the almost universal tradition which characterises rocks and caverns as the haunts and sacred habitations of the Gods; and in consequence of which the form and gloom of such caverns have been universally imitated in the oldest temples. Their external form and appearance is the spiry rock, the towering cliff, and the mountain in its immense extent: How various! how grand! Their inner form, their breaks, and masses, how infinitely more various, grand, and majestic, than any thing which the poor wigwam, and its most ingenious imitations, can suggest or boast of, which, compared to them, dwindle into nothing; their wonderful variety, their shape, their structure, combination of parts, and natural ornaments, depend partly on the difference of the causes and circumstances under which they have been formed, and on the nature of the mountains in which they are found. The Granite, which forms the highest masses of the oldest mountains, affects particular forms, and displays a mixture of parts, which are either not found, or are less discernible in other rocks, such as glittering or gold-coloured mica, chrystal, and a more or less hardened basis, in which these are wrapped up and confined. It is found, evidently stratified, in uncouth beds of immense extent, variously inclined, which furnishes folid maffes of almoft every fize and dimenfion.

The largeft obelifks of Egypt have been hewn out of them. When fhattered or broken by the irrefiftible fhock of earthquakes, the impetuofity of torrents, when worn by the current of rivers, or corroded or mouldered by the flower action of froft, wind, and weather, the horrid crufh and downfall of mountains prefents the granite blocks and ftrata in their rude unwieldy immenfity, wildly piled upon each other, fo as to form, accidentally, huts and caverns beneath. In the fame manner, they appear naked and laid bare on the weather-beaten tops and prominences of the higheft mountains.

The fiffures and divifions of the maffes appear in various directions, agreeably to the force which has acted upon them; and in fome cafes they are wonderfully equipoifed and balanced upon each other.

I have been informed by an ingenious and learned friend of mine, well acquainted with the natural hiftory of Cornwall, that we need not go to Upper Egypt or the Alps for the ftudy of granite mountains; the whole fouth-wefterly end of this ifland, beginning at Dartmoor in Devonfhire, and extending through the whole county of Cornwall, to the remoteft cliffs and rocks of the Scilly Iflands,

is more or lefs a mafs of granite, almoft every where inter-
fected by metallic veins; that this chiefly appears in St. Mi-
chael's Mount, in Mount's Bay, on the fouth coaft; that
fome metallic veins or lodes, in the high towering cliffs on
the north coaft, corroded and decompofed by the furious
battering of the fea, have left ftupendous caverns and excavations, of which he mentions one in Wicka Cove, between
St. Ives and St. Juft, as particularly grand, and worthy the
infpection of the artift, as well as of the natural hiftorian.

IN calcareous, moftly ftratified mountains, caverns are more
various and common: befides the accidental caves produced
by the giving way and tumbling down of mountainous
maffes, and the decompofition of metallic and other lodes,
more extenfive and fingular excavations are found in them,
evidently produced by earthquakes, or by the decompofition
of parts of the rocky maffes, or of the ftratified rock falt,
which they furrounded and covered. Such are, I am informed,
among many others, the caverns near Chudleigh and Ply-
mouth, in Devonfhire, and thofe which are fo juftly famous near Caftleton and Buxton, in Derbyfhire. In thefe
laft we behold the undeniable prototype of the lofty femicircular dome, and of the arched vault, of which the hut of
the Grecians could not fuggeft the idea. I defcribe them,
from the accurate obfervations of the above mentioned ingenious gentleman, as wonderfully regular, and as large coni-
cal excavations in the roof of thefe caverns, which examined

by the light of torches appeared to refemble fo many femicircular or parabolical cupolas, or, to ufe a lefs dignified comparifon, fo many immenfe bells. The caverns in calcareous, or more modern adventitious mountains, fhew in their walls, befides the texture and ftratification, petrified marine, or other bodies, which are never found in granite or fimilar filicious ftones; a wonderful variety of glittering fpar cryftals; and, in particular, incruftations of fnow-white fpar or ftalactite, which either form undulated hangings on their fides, or icicles dripping from their roofs in the fhape of columns, pillars, &c. Thefe are the peculiar glories and features of the grotto of Antiparos. I pafs over the caverns in flate and the loofer grit-ftone, to dwell one inftant longer on thofe which are produced by volcanic eruptions, and chiefly by the contraction of cooling lavas. They totally differ in form and features from the preceding: the forms which thefe affume will refemble the apertures and bubbles which are found in other fcoria. Some of them which are found in Iceland will hold numerous flocks of fheep; they are fpread hundreds of fathoms in various branches under ground, and have ferved formerly as ftrong holds and habitations to the ruftic heroes and warriors, whofe names are highly celebrated in the traditional hiftory and fongs of that country. Fingal's famous and magnificent grotto is a large ftratum of columnar bafaltes, in the ifle of Staffa, though probably it never was fit for habitation, and ftill lefs what fome philofophers have fuppofed it to be, the prototype of the column. That caverns in the loofer chalk, grit-ftone, and beds of hardened volcanic afhes, or tufa, are exceedingly improveable; and that caverns have been inhabited and varioufly improved, is, I think, undeniably evident, from what we fee and read in the monuments and antiquities of every part of the world, and particularly from the immenfe excavated works in the ifland of Salfett, on the coaft of Malabar, and many others.

The eafy tafk of fpecific hiftorical proof I muft leave to others; and requeft my readers juft to confider, that when enlarged and improved natural caverns in rocks and mountains became infufficient to the increafing numbers of men and families, their improvement and enlargement, whatever it might have been, muft naturally bring on imitations of their forms, by artificial excavations of rocks, or artificial grottos, caverns, and catacombs, by the piling up of loofe and moveable natural ftones; and, laftly, by the compofition of brick, or other artificial imitations of natural ftones, which of courfe would produce walls, huts, and houfes of ftone, mud, or brick, and nearly of the fame form.

One natural inference may and ought to be drawn from what has been faid, that the feveral fpecies of ftone buildings, which have been brought more or lefs to perfection, (I mean the Egyptian, Hindoo, Moorifh, and Gothic architecture) inftead of being copies of each other, are actually and effentially the fame; the fpontaneous produce of genius in different countries; the neceffary effects of fimilar neceffity and materials; older and younger brothers and sisters of the same family, conceived, brought up, and bred to more or less grandeur, elegance and perfection, in the Egyptian, Hindoo, and other artificial grottos and caverns. The pyramid, the obelisk, the spire steeple and minaret, are evidently bold, stupendous imitations of the romantic forms of spiry, towering rocks, which the imitators of humble huts never presumed to attempt. The flat roof hundred pillared Egyptian temple, the Indian pagoda, and choultry, are as evident copies of the numerous caverns, cool grottos, and excavations in the rocky banks of the Nile in Upper Egypt, and in the island of Elephanta and Salset near Bombay. Gloom and darkness are common and desirable to both; for Fancy works best when involved in the veil of obscurity. The arched vault and lofty dome was not suggested to the Egyptians and oldest Hindoos by the grotto and sacred caverns in granite mountains; they are the natural forms of other caverns, and in particular the boast, the strength, and glory of more modern Moorish and Gothic temples. If the single or grouped pillars, in many of the props and supports of artificial caverns, should appear heavy, they must be regarded as having been originally props to mountains; and such would be retained in common use, till experience found out easier and more pleasing proportions; and till aspiring genius, at the sight of airy and lofty caverns, dared to give them lightness, and all the fanciful forms and graces of the Gothic style.

Such are my sentiments on the origin of these different modes of architecture. The Grecian confessedly was suggested by the primitive form of a rural hut in a champaign woody country; and the Oriental and Gothic I conceive has derived its form and its ornaments from those surprizing excavations which are found in rocky and mountainous regions. In India these heterogeneous species of building are seldom found combined; and I mention the instance which gave rise to this discussion as very singular indeed. By what means this unnatural union has taken place it is impossible to determine; and conjecture would only lead us astray from the object of these pages, which is a narrative and description of facts.

CHAP. V.

Ceremony of Widows devoting themselves on the Funeral Pile of their Husbands—Minute Description of the Performance of that horrid Sacrifice—Journey to Bidjegur—Description of the Fort, &c.—Arrival at Bauglepoor—The Author accompanies Mr. Cleveland through a Part of his District—Excellent Conduct of Mr. Cleveland in civilizing the Mountaineers—Curious Sacrifice.

WHILE I was pursuing my professional labours in Benares, I received information of a ceremony which was to take place on the banks of the river, and which greatly excited my curiosity. I had often read and repeatedly heard of that most horrid custom amongst, perhaps, the most mild and gentle of the human race, the Hindoos; the sacrifice of the wife on the death of the husband, and that by a means from which nature seems to shrink with the utmost abhorrence, by burning. Many instances of this practice have been given by travellers; those whom I have met with only mention it as taking place among the highest classes of society, whose vanity united with superstitious prejudices might have dictated the circumstance; and I confess I could not entertain any other ideas, when I observed the theatrical parade that seemed to attend it. Mr. Holwell, in his curious work entitled Hiftorical Events relative to India, thus accounts for this more than inhuman practice : " At the demife of the mortal part of the Hindoo great law-giver and prophet, Bramah, his wives, inconfolable for his lofs, refolved not to furvive him, and offered themfelves voluntary victims on his funeral pile. The wives of the chief Rajahs, the firft officers of the ftate, being unwilling to have it thought that they were deficient in fidelity and affection, followed the heroic example fet them by the wives of Bramah. The Bramins, a tribe then newly eftablifhed by their great legiflator, pronounced and declared, that the fpirits of thofe heroines immediately ceafed from their tranfmigrations, and had entered the firft boboon of purification: it followed, that their wives claimed a right of making the fame facrifice of their mortal forms to God, and the manes of their deceafed hufbands. The wives of every Hindoo caught the enthufiaftic (now pious) flame. Thus the heroic acts of a few women brought about a general cuftom. The Bramins had given it the ftamp of religion, and inftituted the forms and ceremonials that were to accompany the facrifice, fubject to reftriction, which leave it a voluntary act of glory, piety, and fortitude." The author proceeds to ftate exprefsly, that he has been prefent at many of thefe facrifices, and particularly and minutely records one that happened on the 4th of February, 1742-3, near to Coffimbuzar, of a young widow between feventeen and eighteen years of age, leaving at fo early an age three children, two boys and a girl; the eldeſt he mentions as not then being four years of age. This infatuated heroine was ſtrongly urged to live, for the future care of her infants; but notwithſtanding this, though the agonies of death were painted to her in the ſtrongeſt and moſt lively terms, ſhe, with a calm and reſolved countenance, put her finger into the fire, and held it there a confiderable time; ſhe then with one hand put fire in the palm of the other, ſprinkled incenſe on it, and fumigated the Bramins. She was then given to underſtand, by ſome of her friends, that ſhe would not be permitted to burn herſelf, and this intimation appeared to give her deep affliction for a few moments; after which ſhe reſolutely replied, that death was in her own power, and that if ſhe was not allowed to burn, according to the principles of her caſt, ſhe would ſtarve herſelf. Her friends, finding her thus peremptory, were obliged at laſt to conſent to the dreadful ſacrifice of this lady, who was of high rank.

The perſon whom I ſaw was of the Bhyſe (merchant) tribe or caſt; a claſs of people we ſhould naturally ſuppoſe exempt from the high and impetuous pride of rank, and in whom the natural defire to preſerve life ſhould in general predominate, undiverted from its proper courſe by a proſpect of poſthumous fame. I may add, that theſe motives are greatly ſtrengthened by the exemption of this claſs from that infamy with which the refuſal is inevitably branded in their ſuperiors. Upon my repairing to the ſpot, on the banks of the river, where the ceremony was to take place, I found the body of the man on a bier, and covered with linen, already brought down and laid at the edge of the river. At this time, about ten in the morning, only a few people were affembled, who appeared deftitute of feeling at the cataftrophe that was to take place; I may even fay that they difplayed the moft perfect apathy and indifference. After waiting a confiderable time the wife appeared, attended by the Bramins, and mufic, with fome few relations. The proceffion was flow and folemn; the victim moved with a fteady and firm ftep; and, apparently with a perfect compofure of countenance, approached clofe to the body of her hufband, where for fome time they halted. She then addreffed thofe who were near her with compofure, and without the leaft trepidation of voice or change of countenance. She held in her left hand a cocoa nut, in which was a red colour mixed up, and dipping in it the fore-finger of her right hand fhe marked thofe near her, to whom fhe wifhed to fhew the laft act of attention. As at this time I ftood clofe to her, fhe obferved me attentively, and with the colour marked me on the forehead. She might be about twenty-four or five years of age, a time of life when the bloom of beauty has generally fled the cheek in India; but ftill fhe preferved a fufficient fhare to prove that fhe muft have been handfome: her figure was fmall, but elegantly turned; and the form of her hands and arms was particularly beautiful. Her drefs was a loofe robe of white flowing drapery, that extended from her head to the feet. The place of sacrifice was higher up on the bank of the river, a hundred yards or more from the spot where we now stood. The pile was composed of dried branches, leaves, and rushes, with a door on one side, and arched and covered on the top: by the side of the door stood a man with a lighted brand. From the time the woman appeared to the taking up of the body to convey it into the pile, might occupy a space of half an hour, which was employed in prayer with the Bramins, in attentions to those who stood near her, and conversation with her relations. When the body was taken up she followed close to it, attended by the chief Bramin; and when it was deposited in the pile, she bowed to all around her, and entered without speaking. The moment she entered, the door was closed; the fire was put to the combustibles, which instantly flamed, and immense quantities of dried wood and other matters were thrown upon it. This last part of the ceremony was accompanied with the shouts of the multitude, who now became numerous, and the whole seemed a mass of confused rejoicing. For my part I felt myself actuated by very different sentiments: the event that I had been witness to was such, that the minutest circumstance attending it could not be erased from my memory; and when the melancholy which had overwhelmed me was somewhat abated, I made a drawing of the subject, and from a picture since painted the annexed plate was engraved.

IN other parts of India, as the Carnatic, this dreadful cuſtom is accompanied in the execution of it with ſtill greater horror. It is aſſerted, that they dig a pit, in which is depoſited a large quantity of combuſtible matter, which is ſet on fire, and the body being let down, the victim throws herſelf into the flaming maſs. In other places, a pile is raiſed extremely high, and the body with the wife is placed upon it, and then the whole is ſet on fire. Whatever is the means, reaſon and nature ſo revolt at the idea, that, were it not a well known and well authenticated circumſtance, it would hardly obtain credit. In truth, I cannot but confeſs, that ſome degree of incredulity was mingled with curioſity on this occaſion; and the deſire of aſcertaining ſo extraordinary a fact was my greateſt inducement to be a ſpectator.

THE war which had commenced in this province in Auguſt was not compleatly finiſhed by the month of October, although the Rajah had left the country, and joined the army of the Mahrattas under Madajee Scindia. The ſtrong fortreſs of Bidjegur yet held out againſt the troops commanded by Major Popham; and I was happy to receive the commands of Mr. Haſtings to proceed to Bidjegur to make drawings of that, and of the fort of Lutteefpoor on the road.

AFTER paſſing the open country, (the cultivation of which had ſuffered but in a ſmall degree from the recent

PROCESSION of a HINDOO WOMAN to the Funeral Pile of her HUSBAND.

Engraved by W. Skelton, from a Picture painted by W. Hodges, R.A.

London Published by J. Edwards, Pall Mall, Jan.º 1793.

INDIA.

disturbances) the traveller enters the jungles or woods, which surround the fort of Lutteefpoor. The woods are chiefly composed of Bamboos, which come close to the walls of the fort, and are so very thick as in some parts to be impenetrable. The fort is built of stone, with the walls flanked with round towers, and is in a ruinous state. Two miles from the fort is a high and difficult rocky pass, at the top of which the country continues level and flat, until nearly within three or four miles of Bidjegur, when it sinks, and there appears a natural fosse surrounding the extremity of the mountain, and the view is terminated in a low swampy country, which, in the time of the rains, is overflowed. Between Lutteefpoor and Bidjegur are considerable woods, intermixed with cultivated ground, and a few villages. Bidjegur is fifty miles from Benares, and the fort is seated on the top of a high mountain, covered from its base to its summit with wood. This is the last of a long range of mountains, which, at this place, rudely decline to the plain. Here I enjoyed an opportunity which falls to the lot of but few professional men in my line; I mean that of observing the military operations of a siege. The camp was formed nearly four miles from the fort: there was, however, a rock about the heighth of the top of the mountains, and within gun shot, commanding one face of the fort, which was square. From this station the walls were battered; and, after a practicable breach was made, the garrison thought fit to surrender. In the garrison were found the mother and other female relatives of

Cheyt Sing, to whom every delicate attention was paid. A View of Bidjegur, taken on the fpot, is fubjoined.

Soon after Bidjegur was taken, preparations were made for the departure of the party attending the Governor General; and towards the end of December we failed, and arrived at Bauglepoor early in January, 1782. As at this place it was my intention to remain for fome time, I took my leave for the prefent of the gentlemen attending the Governor General, who, in the fpace of two months out of the, fix fince we had left Calcutta, had been witnefs to a revolt that had nearly fhaken the Britifh power in India to its bafe; but, by the vigorous exertions of the officers, feconded by the courage and perfeverance of the troops, under a well regulated plan for the recovery of the power of the Eaft India Company, every thing terminated in a manner that ferved to imprefs the powers then at war with the Englifh with the moft formidable opinion of the vigour and energy of the Britifh government. The conduct and gallantry of both officers and troops, in the hour of their utmoft diftrefs, were not improbably a means of facilitating the permanent peace with the Mahratta powers, and particularly with Madajee Scindia, which immediately followed.

Soon after the departure of the gentlemen, about the end of January, Mr. Cleveland propofed to me to accompany him through a part of the diftrict into the hills, to

A VIEW OF BIDJEGUR.

which I readily acceded; and early in February we set out on a tour through a part of the country called the Jungle Terry, to the westward of Bauglepoor. This interior part of the country consists of much wood, intermixed with cultivated ground, and many villages, chiefly inhabited by husbandmen. Among others, I could not but notice the village of Barkope, adjacent to which are many hills, rising almost to the consequence of mountains, and every one of them is insulated by the plain country. The appearance of this part of the country is very singular, having immense masses of stone piled one on another; from the interstices of which are very large timber trees growing out, in some places overshadowing the whole of the rocks: the trees are of various kinds. In many of these rocks I found the teek, a timber remarkable for its hardness and size; and this accompanied with the mango, no less remarkable for its softness, and which produces the fine fruit of that name. The tamarind and other trees are also produced here. On some of the highest of these hills I observed durgaws, or burial places, with little chapels annexed, belonging to the Mussulmans.

In the course of our journey Mr. Cleveland received an invitation from some principal hill chiefs, to the ceremony of an annual sacrifice, which he accepted; and after the business was executed which brought him into this part of his district, we proceeded to the village on the mountain where the ceremony was to take place. The people from whom Mr. Cleveland had received the invitation refide in a range of hills which lie to the fouth and to the weftward of Bauglepoor, extending fouth to the back of Rajemahel. It has been conjectured by fome (how well founded I know not) that this people are the aboriginal natives of the country. They have manners certainly different from the Hindoos, being neither divided into cafts nor tribes, and eating of every fpecies of provifion which the followers of Bramah cannot, as they are limited in this article according to their caft. As it is extremely difficult to decide on the claims of different tribes to antiquity, I could not help fufpecting that thefe may have been formerly no other than the outcafts from the Hindoos, who forming themfelves into a fociety in the receffes of the country, and pofting themfelves in the more mountainous parts, to prevent being furprized, occafionally iffued to commit depredations on the defencelefs people in the plains. On this account, indeed, they became fo formidable, that the Hindoo, Moorifh, and afterwards the Englifh governments, have at all times been under the neceffity of ftationing troops, to check their inroads. Like thofe of all other favages, their incurfions have been merely predatory, and what they feize is by furprize. They generally entered the villages at night, and, murdering the hufbandmen, drove off the cattle, and then fecured themfelves in their fortreffes in the hills. As they were only armed with bows and arrows and a fabre, they were unable either to attack or to withftand regular troops with fire arms. By lying in wait like a tyger in the woods, they frequently cut off the traveller or ſtragglers, and from parties which had been ſent to chaſtiſe them—nor could they, at any time, be induced to reform from their horrid practices, by the moſt vigorous exertions of the military againſt them, until the time Mr. Cleveland was placed at the head of the diſtrict, whoſe judgment ſuggeſted a plan, which a ſhort time afterwards was carried into effect with the happieſt ſucceſs.

It was the humanity of that gentleman, added to the deſire of improving the revenue of this part of his diſtrict for the Company's benefit, that induced him to venture into the hills, alone and unarmed, where he convened ſome of the principal Chiefs; and after the fulleſt aſſurance of his moſt peaceable intentions and good-will towards them, he invited them to viſit him at his reſidence at Bauglepoor. The confidence which he manifeſted in their honour, by truſting to it for his perſonal ſafety, effectually gained their eſteem, and ſome time after a deputation of their Chiefs waited on him. By a variety of attentions, by little preſents, and acts of perſonal kindneſs, he ſo ſubdued their ferocious ſpirits, that they promiſed to deſiſt entirely from their uſual depredations; and returning to their families and their people, the whole body became earneſt to be perſonally introduced to this humane and benevolent ſtranger. Mr. Cleveland had by this time digeſted his plan, which he brought forwards by degrees, and whatever he propoſed they inſtantly agreed to.

He sent presents to their wives, and wherever he saw he caressed their children, decorating them with beads; and to their Chiefs he presented medals, as a mark of his friendship, and as a reward for their improving civilization. At length, when he found them prepared for the accomplishment of his plan, he ordered cloaths to be made, like those of the Seapoys in the Company's service for a few, he furnished them with firelocks, and they became regularly drill'd. Vain of their newly acquired knowledge, these new soldiers soon imparted the enthusiasm to the rest of the nation, who earnestly petitioned for the same distinction. Thus, at their own request, a battalion was formed for the preservation of good order, and in less than two years, he had a fine corps of these people embodied, for the express purpose of preserving from injury the very country that had for centuries before been the scene of their depredations. A camp was formed for a corps of a thousand men, three miles from Bauglepoor, where their families resided with them, and where strict military discipline was observed. Thus the ingenuity, address, and humanity of one man effected, in the space of little more than two years, more than could even have been hoped for from the utmost exertions of military severity.

AFTER leaving the village of Barkope, which is nearly in the centre of the Jungleterry, and travelling through the flat country, crossing a small river, we entered the hills, which are covered with wood, and from the summits of several had beautiful and extensive prospects, mostly diversified by the meandering of the Ganges, and by the varied face of the country, to a great extent, from the eastern shore.

Though the space which we travelled in this route was not great, the serpentine road, the closeness of the woods, and, in many places, the extreme steepness of the hills occasioned considerable heat and fatigue. On the second day of our journey, we arrived at the village on the hill, where the ceremony was to take place: here Mr. Cleveland was received with every mark of respect and affection by the chiefs who were already assembled, and even the women and the children contended who should be the most forward in expressing their regard.

They had built a small open hut in the village, purposely for his reception, and the following morning every person in the neighbourhood was collected to be present at the annual sacrifice.

The ceremony took place about nine o'clock. Before a small hut, and about six feet from the ground, was raised a kind of altar made of bamboos. The grand sacrifice was preceded by the decolation of a kid and a cock, the heads of which were thrown upon the altar, and there remained: little attention however was paid to this part of the ceremony by any of the party present. An hour or more afterwards, we were apprised that the principal rite was about to be performed, and we repaired in confequence, without lofs of time, to the place of rendezvous.

The people had purchafed a fine large buffaloe, which they had fattened, and were now dragging with ropes, by the horns, towards the fpot where the kid and the cock had been already facrificed. The animal was brought, with much difficulty, to the place of facrifice, where the chief of the village attended: he was perfectly naked, except a cloth round his middle, and held a large and bright fabre in his hand. The place round the altar was foon crowded with people; men, women, and children attended, and the young men were all perfectly naked. To prevent the efcape of the animal, they firft ham-ftringed him, and then began the dreadful operation. The chief ftood on the left fide of the animal, and with his fabre ftriking the upper part of the neck, near to the fhoulder, muft have given exquifite pain to the poor animal, who expreffed it with great violence, by writhing, bellowing, and ftruggling with thofe that held him; indeed, their utmoft exertions were fcarcely fufficient to prevent him from breaking away. This horrid bufinefs continued for the fpace of more than a quarter of an hour, before the fpine of the neck was cut through. When the animal fell, the Melchifadeck of the day ftill continued his work, and it was fome time before the head was perfectly feparated. Previous to the laft ftroke, he feemed to paufe, and an univerfal filence reigned: when this was given, he ſtood perfectly erect, and, by raiſing the arm which held the ſabre to the utmoſt extenſion, ſeemed to give the ſignal to the multitude, who ruſh'd in and began ſcooping up the blood of the animal, which had liberally flowed from him on the ground. This they drank up, mixed as it was with the duſt and loam, and beſmeared each other with their hands. Bodies of them ruſhed over bodies, and rolling in confuſed heaps, they appeared like an aſſemblage of demons or bacchanals in their moſt frantic moments. The body was next cut to pieces, and devoured; the head, however, was reſerved, as thoſe of the kid and the cock: ſo various are men in their conceptions concerning what may be moſt acceptable to the Deity. After the completion of this ſacrifice, they retired to their ſeveral habitations in parties, and began the rejoicing of the day, which, indeed, was devoted to univerſal revelling and intoxication; and I could have wiſhed, for the honour of the fair ſex, that theſe latter exceſſes had been confined to the men. After the rites of Bacchus had far exceeded the bounds of temperance, thoſe who were capable of ſuſtaining an erect poſition began dancing, men and women promiſcuouſly; others, in parties, roared out their extravagant joy in ſuch ſtrains, as may be ſuppoſed adapted to the preſent ſtate of the performers; and the night concluded with a dead ſilence.

MR. Cleveland did not remain long after the performance of the ceremony; we therefore proceeded on our journey back to Bauglepoor, and on the following day arrived at Deogur, a small village, famous for the resort of Hindoo pilgrims, this being a sacred spot. There are five curious Pagodas here, of perhaps the very oldest construction to be found in India. They are simply pyramids, formed by putting stone on stone, the apex is cut off at about one seventh of the whole height of the complete pyramid, and four of them have small ornamental buildings on the top, evidently of more modern work, which are finished by an ornament made of copper, and gilt, perfectly resembling the trident of the Greek Neptune. These Pagodas have each a small chamber in the center of twelve feet square, with a lamp, hanging over the Lingham*. The passage to it is exactly of a heighth and width sufficient to admit one person. This chamber can have no light from without, but what enters from the door and through the passage.

At Deogur multitudes of pilgrims are seen, who carry the water of the Ganges to the western side of the peninsula of India. The water is carried in large flasks or bottles, holding nearly five quarts each, suspended at either end of a bamboo, which rests upon the shoulders. A considerable trade is carried on by these people, and the price of the holy water bears a proportion to the distance of the place where it is sold from the river.

* The Lingham is the great object of superstition among the followers of Brahmah, it being the general symbol of renovative nature.

OUR return was so nearly in the direction in which we came, that no opportunity was offered for any new obfervations; indeed this part of the country does not abound in objects of curiofity. In the great famine which raged through Indoftan in the year 1770, and the ravages of which were particularly felt in every part of Bengal, the Jungleterry is faid to have fuffered greatly. I have underftood that it was before this time highly cultivated, and filled with induftrious hufbandmen and manufacturers, and the population was eftimated at more than eighteen thoufand people. It is, however, at prefent reduced to a few hundreds, great numbers having been cut off by famine, and others having emigrated in fearch of food. The filence that reigns here, owing to this depopulation, fpreads a melancholy over the mind of the traveller, and for miles together, nothing is heard but the fcreams of the cormorant, nor is the trace of any footfteps found but thofe of the wild elephant. On my return to Bauglepoor, converfing on this fubject with my friend, I mentioned the popular impreffions that had gone forth at, and after that melancholy period, and expreffing my feelings on the fubject, not without feverity againft fome leading characters, then in Bengal, and who had been accufed of taking advantage of the public diftrefs for the accumulation of large private fortunes; he with his ufual candour and regard to juftice, explained the conduct of certain gentlemen, who had very unjuftly fuffered in their character, by malignant infinuations, and fhewed me, from the archives of the diſtrict, written documents collected at the time, which convinced me that the gentlemen, who then reſided in public characters at Moorſhedabad, and at Bauglepoor, and other ſurrounding diſtricts, where the famine raged in its utmoſt violence, had taken and employed every means that liberality and benevolence, under the direction of ability, could poſſibly ſuggeſt for the preſervation of the poor, and many of them at the expence of their own private fortunes. I ſhould not have touched upon this ſubject, but from a motive of ſtrict juſtice, as few perſons have had an opportunity of inſpecting the proofs and records which Mr. Cleveland indulged me with a ſight of.

CHAP. VI.

The Author returns to Calcutta—Seized with a dangerous Illnefs—Recovery—Proceeds on a new Tour—Route from Calcutta to Allahabad—Defcription of the Fort and Town —Cawnpoor—Lucknow, Defcription of that City—Palace of the Nabob—Journey to Fyzabad and Oud—Defcription of the City of Fyzabad—Palace of Sujah ul Dowlah— Oud, &c.

AFTER remaining about four months at Bauglepoor, having completed my bufinefs, I proceeded for Calcutta, where I arrived on the 15th of May, 1782, and immediately after proceeded in thofe works I had undertaken. The extreme heat at this feafon, however, added to an affiduous application to my profeffion, threw me into a violent fever; and, after my recovery from the difeafe, I continued very weak for a long time.

IN this ftate of debility I had it frequently in contemplation to proceed to Europe; but the cool weather returning towards the end of November, my ftrength and vigour gradually returned with it. I felt all my curiofity revived; and once more refolved to indulge my inclination to vifit other parts of India. With this view, I explained to the Governor

General my wiſhes to viſit Agra, &c. &c. and I had the honour of receiving his ſanction, and that of the Council. On the 10th of January, 1783, I began my journey by land, paſſing once more through Moorſhedabad, Bauglepoor, Mongheir, and Patna, to Benares. As I had not ſtopped at any of the above places, except Bauglepoor, where I remained only one day, I found myſelf conſiderably fatigued by a journey of nearly five hundred miles, in a pallankeen; I therefore determined to reſt at Benares, and was happy to receive the civilities of Mr. Markham, the Reſident, a gentleman univerſally known for his liberality and accompliſhments.

HAVING prolonged my ſtay four days, and finding myſelf perfectly recruited, I purſued my journey, and arrived at Allahabad on the ſecond day after I left Benares. This is the point of confluence of the two great rivers Jumna and Ganges; and between the eaſtern boundaries of the Jumna and the weſtern boundaries of the Ganges is the country known by the name of Dooab, or a country lying between two rivers, the whole of which is eſteemed very fertile. Immediately at the point is the fort of Allahabad, built entirely of ſtone, by the great Emperor Acbar; and commanding, from its ſituation, the navigation of both rivers; a circumſtance which ought to make it a place of conſequence, although it is now left to ruin. It is built in the old ſtyle of fortification, with walls flanked by round and square towers; and that which is called the Agra gate, pointing towards Agra, is very handsome, being ornamented with many small pavilions on the top; and having within the exterior gate two other gates, which were formerly secured with portcullies. The fort covers a considerable space of ground, and must have required a great number of men for its protection. Within the walls of the fort are large areas; in one of which I observed a small monument over the tomb of an English officer; the inscription, however, was nearly defaced. These areas are now no more than heaps of ruins, chiefly covered with the dust of the crumbled buildings. This was one of the many fortresses that extended nearly in a line from Lahore to Chunar Gur, on the Ganges, all of which were raised by Acbar, and must have secured the empire from the confines of Persia to the borders of Bengal. Without the fort is what is called the city; consisting, however, merely of thatched huts, and with scarcely a vestige of any considerable house remaining. This place is now in the possession of Asoph ul Dowlah, Nabob of Oud: it was, for some time, the residence of the present Great Mogul, the unfortunate Shah Allum, after his unsuccessful attack, and his loss of the battles of Geriah and Buxar, where he attended the late Nabob Sujah ul Dowlah, and on the loss of which he threw himself on the protection of the English, by whose influence and power Allahabad and the adjoining province of Korah were allotted him for his support.

TRAVELS IN

DURING a stay of three days I made several drawings of the fort, and then proceeded to Cawnpoor, a large military station on the Ganges. This is a cantonment for a brigade, amounting, on the war establishment, to ten thousand men; and may be considered as a great encampment, the men living in huts with their families instead of tents.

CROSSING the Ganges at this place, I continued my progress to Lucknow, where I arrived on the 25th of January. The distance from Calcutta to this place is commonly said to be, by the route through Benares, nearly nine hundred miles; but this estimate is certainly too great. Major Rennell, whose authority must be considered as absolute, determines it to be 650 miles, by the nearest road. It is well known that this city is at present the capital of the province of Oud, and the residence of Asoph ul Dowlah, the Nabob, who is also Vizier of the remaining part of the empire of the Great Mogul. The city is extensive, but meanly built: the houses are chiefly mud walls, covered with thatch, and many consist entirely of mats and bamboos, and are thatched with leaves of the cocoa nut, palm tree, and sometimes with straw. Very few, indeed, of the houses of the natives are built with brick: the streets are crooked, narrow, and the worst I have seen in India. In the dry season the dust and heat are intolerable; in the rainy season the mire is so deep, as to be scarcely passable; and there are a great number of elephants, belonging to the Nabob and the great men of his court, which are continually paffing the ftreets, either to the palace, or to the river, to the great danger and annoyance of the foot paffenger, as well as the inferior clafs of fhopkeepers. The comforts, the convenience, or the property of this clafs of people are, indeed, little attended to, either by great men or their fervants; the elephant himfelf is frequently known to be infinitely more attentive to them as he paffes, and to children in particular.

The palace of the Nabob is on a high bank, near to the river, and commanding an extenfive view both of the Goomty and the country on the eaftern fide. A fmall part of it was raifed by the late Nabob Sujah ul Dowlah, the father of Afoph ul Dowlah. It has, however, been greatly extended by the prefent prince, who has erected large courts within the walls, and a durbar, where he receives publickly all perfons that are prefented. This durbar is a range of three arcades, parallel to each other, and fupported by columns in the Moorifh ftyle: the ceiling, and the whole of this, is beautifully gilt, and painted with ornaments and flowers. It is afcended by fteps from a flower garden, laid out in the fame manner as we fee in Indian paintings, which are all in fquare plats, in which are planted flowers of the ftrongeft fcent; fo ftrong, indeed, as to be offenfive at firft to the nerves of a European. The exterior of the building is not to be commended: it reminded me of what I had imagined might be the ftyle of a Baron's caftle in Europe, about the twelfth century. Clofe to the palace, divided by a narrow dirty or dufty road, is a garden, lately made by the Nabob, walled round, and at each angle is a grand pavilion, built of brick, and covered with chunam or ftucco, and then painted with ornaments, which at a little diftance has a rich effect. I have introduced a View of the Palace: on the foreground of the picture is one of the pavilions, and on a high bank is a mofque, with two minarets; and adjoining is a durgaw, or burial place, with a view of the river. The picture from which the print was engraved was painted on the fpot.

As at this time Major Brown was appointed on an embaffy to Mirza Shuffy Khawn, and was to proceed immediately on his miffion through a part of the country which I intended to vifit, I wrote to that gentleman, fignifying my wifhes to accompany him; as I knew that under the protection of his public character I fhould experience no inconvenience from the fufpicions of the people with refpect to my purfuits; and as in his anfwer I found he was not to be at Etawah until the ninth of February, I determined, in the interim, to make a journey to Fyzabad and the ancient city of Oud. I was affifted in this by Mr. Briftow, the then Refident at Lucknow; and immediately on the receipt of Major Brown's letter I fet out on my journey, and arrived at Fyzabad on the fecond day; a diftance of forty cofs, or eighty Englifh miles, in a fouth-eaft direction. As the Refident at Lucknow had writ-

A VIEW of the PALACE of the NABOB ASOPH ul DOWLAH at LUCKNOW.

Engraved by Jn.º Miller from a picture painted by W. Hodges R.A
in the Collection of Warren Hastings Esq.ʳ

Published by J. Edwards, Pall Mall, Jan.ʸ 1791.

ten to an officer in the fervice of the Nabob, refiding at Fyzabad, I was received at my entrance into the city by a perfon, who was ordered to fhew the pallankeen bearers to a fmall houfe in a large garden, which was allotted for my accommodation during my ftay.

The city of Fyzabad is of confiderable extent, and appears to contain a great number of people, chiefly of the loweft clafs; for the court being removed to Lucknow, drew after it the great men, and the moft eminent of the merchants, bankers, and fhroffs, or money-changers. Thefe laft are perfons in all the towns, and even villages, who make large fums by their knowledge of the exchange, which in India is in a ftate of conftant fluctuation, to the great injury of the poor and the induftrious.

The private luxury and vices of the Muffulman princes too frequently reduce them to a ftate of real poverty, even with large revenues; and too often they delegate to artful, defigning, and avaricious characters, the management and concerns of the ftate, and become virtually the plunderers inftead of the parents of their fubjects. Thefe men, eager after their own private gain, and knowing well that their conduct will not bear the blaze of day, connive at any villainy that may be acted by thofe of inferior degree; many of whom are, indeed, their actual agents. Thus it is that the people at large retain no real regard for their governors, and the natural confequence is, that the princes are frequently left, in the hour of diftrefs, quite deftitute of fupport, and an eafy prey to any invader.

IN the city of Fyzabad there are remains of many handfome brick buildings. That in which I refided has a large and beautiful pavilion over the gateway or principal entrance. The afcent is by a narrow ftair-cafe, which leads to three open rooms, commanding the whole city on the one fide, and on the other the garden and a vaft extent of country, with a view of the river Gogra, which is not far diftant, and which is here a large river. Oppofite the gate is a mofque, (built by the late Nabob) with three domes; the center one is very large. The form of thefe domes is perfectly that of an egg fet on its point: the apparent want of firmnefs at the bafe has, however, a very unpleafant effect on the fpectator; and however difficult it may have been for the architect to produce, the confideration of this circumftance does not make amends for the evident want of elegance, nay almoft of propriety.

SOON after my arrival I was waited upon by a perfon from the mother of the prefent Nabob, accompanied with a number of difhes of various curries, and pillaws, for my refrefhment after the fatigue of my journey, and compliments in the Moorifh ftyle; indeed, fo high and dignified, that I could have almoft fancied myfelf tranformed into an

Indian Nabob. After returning my refpects in the humbleft ftyle, and having taken my repaft, which indeed was excellent, (and would have been better, had it been accompanied with a glafs or two of good wine inftead of water) I proceeded to view the city and the remains of the palace, built by the late Nabob Sujah ul Dowlah. This is a vaft building, covering a great extent of ground, having feveral areas or courts, and many feparate buildings in them. In the inner court are the remains of the durbar, or hall of public audience; an elegant building on the fame plan as that already mentioned in the palace at Lucknow, but much richer: the painting and gilding greatly gone to decay. There are many other buildings defigned for offices, or other accommodations. Within an interior court is a large extent of building, the principal front of which is on the banks of the river; and when it was firft raifed muft have been very handfome. This was the part defigned for the domeftic habitation of the Nabob. Adjoining are other buildings, defigned for the Zananah, and in which are the remnants of the gardens. The grand entrance to the palace is through a large and handfome gate, the fuperftructure of which was a place of arms, and there is ftill a guard kept in it. On the top of the gate was the fituation of the nobut, (a great drum) which is an appendage of royalty in India, and when beaten is heard over a great city. The nobut is ufually beaten at fun-rife and fun-fet. Nearly adjoining Fyzabad are the remains of the very ancient city of Oud, which is said to have been the first imperial city of Hindostan, and to have been built by their hero Krishen. In Colonel Dowe's translation of Feritsha's history, it is mentioned as the capital of a great kingdom, one thousand two hundred and nine years previous to the Christian Æra; and it is frequently mentioned in the famous Hindoo work in Shanscrite, (the learned language of the Bramins) the Mahaberet, under the name of Adjudea. Whatever may have been its former magnificence, however, no traces are now left. It is seated at present on the banks of the Gogra; but, in all probability, many years back was at a considerable distance from it, it being in a line with Fyzabad; for, not many years since, upon the building of the palace, Sujah ul Dowlah is said to have daily offered up prayers that the river might flow nearer it, which it now compleatly does, washing the walls of the principal front.* At this place and Fyzabad I remained a few days to complete my drawings, and returned to Lucknow by the same route as I came. The country I had passed through from Allahabad to Lucknow, and thence to Fyzabad, has the same general character, and there are very few elevations to be seen in it that are considerable. It is in a moderate state of cultivation; in some parts better than others; but

* Oud is considered as a place of sanctity, and the Hindoos consequently perform pilgrimages thither, continually, from all quarters of India.

where it is neglected, it is evidently more from the want of property in the people, than the natural sterility of the country, which, on the contrary, I believe to be capable of producing the finest crops. The villages, of which there are many, some are comfortable in their appearance, and others apparently distressed. After leaving the flourishing district of Benares, I could not help viewing with a melancholy concern the miserable appearance of all the territories which were under the absolute direction of Mussulman tyrants.

CHAP. VII.

*Journey to Etaya—Defcription of that Place—Jefwontnagur
—O'Kraine—Shekoabad—Fyrozabad— Etamadpoor— Shah
Dara—Agra—Magnificent Ruins—Arrival at the Camp of
the Nabob Mirza Shuffy Khawn—A venerable Chief who had
ferved under Kouli Khawn—Maufoleum of Acbar—Taje
Mahael—Futtypoor Sicri—Fortrefs of Gawlior—Return to
Lucknow.*

ON the 10th of February I fet out on my journey to join Major Brown at Etaya. As I travelled by a fet of pallankeen bearers to the number of fifteen, and which had no relief beyond their own fet, my ftages became fhort; particularly fo, as I was now encumbered with baggage, carrying with me a tent, and all the articles for cooking, &c. the number of fervants neceffary for dreffing provifions, &c. makes the train even of an individual confiderable. On the 13th I arrived at the encampment of Major Brown, his tent being pitched clofe to the town of Etaya. The road to this place runs weftward from Lucknow, and the Ganges is croffed nearly midway, and at this feafon of the year is in many places fordable: there is a fordable ftream alfo to the weftward of the Ganges, called Callinuddie, which, however, in the time of the periodical rains is a confiderable river. The country from Lucknow to Etaya is in a moderate ſtate of cultivation, but the villages are poor. Etaya is ſituated on a very high bank of the river Jumna, the ſides of which conſiſt of what in India is called concha, which is originally ſand, but the conſtant action of the ſun in the dry ſeaſon forms it almoſt into a vitrification. Many parts of the banks are ſixty feet high. On the top, near to the river, are the remains of a fort: the town itſelf is all built on the heights, which, as it approaches the river, is divided into a variety of ſeparate hills by deep ravines, made by the rains. The Jumna is at this place a large river, in which are many iſlands of ſand, that are overflowed in the time of the floods. The town is large, but very wretched, having but two tolerable houſes in it.

On the 15th we moved forward to Jeſwontnagur, ſix coſs from Etaya, or near twelve Engliſh miles. It ſhould be obſerved in this place, that the Indian meaſure of a coſs is leſs than in Bengal, the latter being nearly two Engliſh miles; but in the upper parts of Hindoſtan, ſcarcely more than one and a half, as may be ſeen on the ſcale in the map. The country from Etaya to this place is very little cultivated; the villages are not populous, and the few inhabitants appear very wretched.

On the 16th we halted at O'Kraine, ſix coſs further, almoſt at the termination of the Nabob of Oud's country.

THROUGH the whole of the laſt day's journey I obſerved ſcarcely a ſpot in cultivation; the villages, of which there are ſeveral, were in ruins, and the whole preſented almoſt one uninterrupted ſcene of deſolation. On the laſt day's march we met a few unfortunate people paſſing down into the provinces, in order actually to avoid being ſtarved, begging their way. The ſervants we had brought from Bengal with us appearing clean, healthy, and chearful, perhaps rendered the appearance of theſe poor people the more wretched.

ON the 17th I arrived at Shekoabad, which takes its name from Dara Sheko, the eldeſt and moſt unfortunate ſon of the Emperor Shah Iehan, who, in the conteſt for the empire with Aurungzebe, his youngeſt brother, was defeated, hunted down like a wild beaſt, and at laſt taken. When a priſoner, he was ſtripped and ſeated on an elephant, for the deriſion of a conquering army, and was at laſt unmercifully murdered. From O'Kraine to this place there are ſome few ſpots of cultivated ground; and the richneſs and fulneſs of the grain ſufficiently ſhew what the whole of the country is çapable of producing, were it in cultivation.

DURING this day's march our courſe lay through two villages, which were better and cleaner than thoſe we had before paſſed. To the right and the left of our road were many ruined villages; and on every hillock, or riſing ground, are mud forts, or their ruins. This town (for, on the comparison with what we had passed since leaving Etaya, it may be so called) has a considerable number of people, and the adjacent ground is in cultivation. I found here the remains of a hunting seat, built by Dara Sheko, and a tank belonging to it: from the ruins it must have been large. Adjoining the tank is a small grove of palm and other trees; but, except these, there are no trees in the neighbourhood; nor is there any water but from a few wells, and the abovementioned tank, which was nearly dry when I saw it. There are considerable remains of other buildings, in and about the town, some of them apparently on a large scale.

WE continued our route, for six coss, to Fyrozabad, which is a considerable village. Between Shekoabad and Fyrozabad are a few spots of cultivated ground. This village takes its name from the Purgunnah, which is a small district within a larger: it was at this time in the hand of a Gosine, or Hindoo Religious; and as the spirit of the Hindoo government is favourable to agriculture in the highest degree, this spot appeared a perfect garden. It must, indeed, be observed, that although the Hindoo governors or proprietors, from the principle of avarice, may sometimes distress, they do not destroy the endeavours of the poor, as the Mussulmans. For his protection, the Gosine had a camp formed in the neighbourhood, amounting to two thousand men, well armed, and a small park of artillery, in which I saw two fine pieces of battering cannon. The perfons of the men, forming this little army, appeared to me remarkable for their manly beauty and ftature, moft of them being upwards of fix feet in height, and their manners, whilft I was in their camp, were extremely modeft and attentive. On the following day we reached Etamadpoor, a diftance of fix cofs, but found in our journey that, upon leaving the Purgunnah of Firozeabad, the line was ftrongly marked by the wild wafte that enfued.

At Etamadpoor is a fmall building in the center of a large tank, the fides of which are built up with ftone, as is the center building, and a bridge of feveral arches, which communicates with it from the fide of the tank. Around the whole are large mounds of earth, formed from the excavations in making the tank. At this time there was but little water in it.

From this place we had a fight of the fpires of the once fplendid and imperial city of Agra.

On the 23d, at the diftance of five cofs from Etamadpoor, we encamped on the Shah Darah, about a cofs on the eaftern fide of the river Jumna, oppofite the city. The whole of this fpot, as far as the eye can reach, is one general fcene of ruined buildings, long walls, vaft arches, parts of domes, and fome very large buildings, as the Cuttera, built by the great Shah Heft Khawn, in the reign of Aurungzebe; here are alfo feveral Tombs.

ALONG the weftern bank of the river are feen the ruined palaces of the great Omrahs, built in the time of Acbar Jehanguire, and Shah Jehan. A little farther, the city of Agra offers itfelf to the eye, with the great fort and palace, and the profpect is terminated to the fouth-weft by that vaft monument of eaftern elegance, the Taje Mahel, built by the emperor Shah Jehan.

THIS fpot takes its name from Dara, a tent, and Shah, king or fovereign, being the fpot where the emperor's tent was firft fixed, when he made his progrefs from Agra to the eaftern provinces of the empire. It being the general cuftom, from the time the dynafty of the Moguls was fixed in India, under Acbar, that the emperor fhould take the field in the fummer months, with a large army, attended by the whole court, the bankers, and the artifans, &c. Thus the camp became a great city under tents, and each trade had its feveral quarter allotted to them, the emperor's tent being in the center of the whole, furrounded by thofe of the great officers of ftate.

ON the 24th Major Brown was waited upon by Arafiab Khawn, an Omrah of high rank, from the Nabob Mirza Shuffeh Khawn, who lay encamped three cofs to the north-

A VIEW of AGRA taken from the SOUTH WEST.
Engraved by J. Walker, from a Picture Painted by W. Hodges, R.A.
in the Collection of Warren Hastings Esq.

London. Published by J. Edwards, Pall Mall, Jan.y 1.st 1791.

weft of Agra, and to whofe camp we proceeded, croffing the Jumna, and paffed through a part of the city of Agra. On the following day we pitched our tents to the eaftward of the Nabob's encampment, in a garden walled round, and which formerly was adorned with very confiderable buildings, now in ruins; this was a work of Acbar for the accommodation of one of his daughters.

THE camp of Mirza Shuffeh extended over a great fpace of ground, and more refembled a great city than a camp, having fhops of every denomination, retaining in part the charaƈter of the armies of the great emperors, only without their fplendor. The camp was faid to contain forty thoufand men; but it appeared to me that the number was greatly exaggerated. This, however, fhould be added, that every foldier, and every tradefman and artificer, had his family with him. In the park of artillery were forty-two pieces of cannon of various calibers. Some of the largeft guns were French pieces, and very fine ones; but the greater number were very indifferent, the metal much corroded, and the carriages rotten. It is not improbable that the tent of the Nabob might have been formerly an imperial one, being of crimfon velvet, embroidered in many parts with gold, and lined with filk. It was, however, much torn and moth-eaten, and had therefore no very fplendid appearance.

A FEW days after our arrival, I attended Major Brown to the Durbar of the Nabob, where we found the principal commanders, amongſt whom were ſeveral old Perſian Chiefs, with beards depending to their girdles, and countenances of great dignity. One of the hoary Chiefs, I found by his converſation, had attended Nadir Shah, or Thomas Kouli Khan, when he made his famous expedition into Hindoſtan, in the year 1739, and had remained in India ſince that time. The old ſoldier's eye appeared in a flame when he mentioned his name, at the recollection of the actions and victories he had aſſiſted at, or been witneſs to, under his former commander. After the ceremony of reception, which was by touching the turban with the right hand, without riſing from their ſeats, we were deſired to ſit, for which purpoſe there were old faſhioned chairs brought, which had formerly been rich in carved work and velvet, but were now greatly injured by the hand of time; otter and roſe-water were handed round, as a mark of diſtinction. The Nabob Mirza Shuffeh ſat in the center of a ſemicircle, ſurrounded by his Chiefs, with an innumerable crowd of ſervants ſtanding behind. After remaining about half an hour, we retired. This was a viſit of ceremony, and the buſineſs of Major Brown's miſſion was not entered upon for many days afterwards, for, amongſt theſe people, delay ſeems a ſettled principle of etiquette.

WHILST we lay encamped at this place, I made daily excurſions to Agra and the neighbourhood, the weather at this ſeaſon greatly favouring my purſuits. Our journeys were ſhort, and were begun frequently between five and ſix in the morning, fometimes earlier. I had the whole day for my ftudies. The climate at this feafon is delightful, the mornings clear and very cold, frequently frofty, in fo much, that I have feen feveral tanks frozen entirely over; but in the middle of the day we generally found it very hot. I paffed moft of my days at Agra, making drawings either of the great fort or other buildings, moft of which lay in ruins.

THE city of Agra is fituated on the fouth fide of the river Jumna, which at this place is not fordable, and rifes immediately from the water, extending in a vaft femicircle. It is fuppofed to be a place of high antiquity. The prefent city, however, was raifed by the emperor Acbar, about 1566, and named from him Acbarabad, and was the principal feat of his government. The fort, in which is included the imperial palace, is of vaft extent. A view of the fort is given, and is fuch as will afford a general idea of the building and its fituation. It is conftructed of a red free ftone, and it would appear to have been very ftrong, when firft raifed. It originally had a double wet ditch, of great width and depth, and well fupplied from the river. The fort was an ifland, formed by three ditches; one face of it, that to the eaftward, was wafhed to the foot of the walls by the river. The outer ditch is now totally ruined, the high road going through it, as may be obferved in the Plate. The inner ditch is very bad in many places, and in feveral is quite dry. The city was encircled by a wall and towers at a bow-fhot diftance from each other.

SHAH JEHAN, the grandfon of Acbar, difliking the fituation of Agra, from the exceffive heats to which it was expofed in the fummer months, and defirous to raife a metropolis which fhould bear his own name, built a great city adjoining the old one of Dehli, and named it Jehanabad; but the name, like the empire, is now nearly loft. To people his new city, he is faid to have tranfported thither one half of the people of Agra, to the amount of upwards of five hundred thoufand. The ruins that immediately enfued in Agra, rendered it neceffary to erect, for the fecurity of the people, another wall, forming a part of a circle within the old one; and this wall was built by Joy Singh, a Hindoo Raja in the fervice of the emperor Aurungzebe.

THE whole fpace between thefe two walls is one mafs of ruins. The inner wall is but in indifferent repair, and within it is eafy to difcern that it is chiefly compofed from the ruined buildings, except, indeed, towards the Dehli gate of the fort, where is the great Musjüd or Mofque, built of red ftone, but greatly gone to decay. Adjacent to this fpot is the Choke, or Exchange, which is now a mere ruin; and even the fort itfelf, from its having frequently changed its mafters, in the courfe of the laft feventy years, is going rapidly to defolation. It was taken by Colonel Polier, when that gentleman was in the fervice of the Nabob Zoolfeccar ul Dowlah, better known by the name of Nedjif Khawn. In the eaftern front of the fort was the imperial refidence, built of white marble, covered on the top with plates of copper gilt, which to this day retain their full luftre, and at no great diftance there is a Mofque, built of the fame beautiful materials, with copper ornaments and gilt. It was impoffible to contemplate the ruins of this grand and venerable city, without feeling the deepeft impreffions of melancholy. I am, indeed, well informed, that the ruins extend, along the banks of the river, not lefs than fourteen Englifh miles.

The palace of Dara Sheko, built by that prince, includes an extent of ground not lefs than the fquare of Lincoln's-inn fields. It is dangerous even to walk among thefe ruins; for at every ftep, unlefs great care is taken, the paffenger is liable to fink through holes into the covered vaults, which are now the habitation of dangerous reptiles. The ftreets in this city are very narrow, and evidently not laid out on any well directed plan. I went once to a Hummaum, or bath, which had formerly belonged to the palace of one of the great men of the court, as was plain from the expences that had been laid out on it; being lined with the fineft coloured marbles, with many pieces of lapis lazuli introduced amongft the ornaments, which were very beautiful, in the Moorifh ftyle, compofed of mofaic and flowers; the imitations of the latter, I muft add, were remarkably good.

At the diftance of three cofs, or a little more, from Agra, on the great high road leading to Dehli, at a place called

Secundrii, stands the tomb of the emperor Acbar. This enormous building is seated in a garden, regularly planted both with forest and fruit-trees, and many flowering shrubs, and walled round, which is supposed to contain a space of upwards of twenty English acres. The monument is raised in the center of the garden; it is a square building, with gates in the center on each side, and great pavilions at the angles and over the gates: it consists of five several stories, which gradually diminish with pavilions at each angle. The domes of the several pavilions are of white marble, the rest of the building is of red stone, in parts intermixed with white marble. The fifth or upper story is entirely of white marble, and has a range of windows running round each side, which are fret work, cut out of the solid slab. The pavilions that finish this story are likewise of marble; these have been greatly damaged, as I was told, by lightning, and by an earthquake. One of the pavilions is quite gone, and the domes of the others are greatly injured. The inside of this upper story is curiously inlaid with black marble, expressive of certain passages from the Koran; and I was informed by a critic in Persian writing, that it is in the most perfect style. On each story of this building are large terrasses, which, in the times of the emperors Jehanguire and Jehan, had coverings of gold cloth, supported by pillars of silver. Under the shade of these awnings the mollahs or priests of the religion of Mahommed conversed with men of learning.

THE principal entrance is by a grand gate leading to the garden; the front highly ornamented with mofaics of different coloured marbles, inlaid in copartments. On either fide the center are two ftories of pointed arches, and large receffes; in the upper ftory is a door in the center, and a window over it, with a balluftrade in front; the lower receffes have one window in each. In the center is one vaft pointed arch; and this part of the building rifes very confiderably above the fide over the two ftories which have been juft defcribed. On the top, and fomewhat behind the front of this part of the building, raifed on fquare columns, are two farcophagi of black marble; and two others immediately behind the back front of the gate, anfwering to thofe in the principal front. At each angle of the gate (this building being an oblong fquare) are minarets of white marble, rifing to a great heighth, in part fluted; above the flutes, half way up the minarets, are balluftrades; and there is likewife one near the top. Thefe minarets were formerly crowned with open pavilions, and finifhed with domes, which have long fince been deftroyed. In thefe minarets are ftaircafes, leading to the two balconies that furround them. A large print, by that excellent artift Mr. Brown, has been engraved and publifhed from a picture of this gate, which gives a more perfect idea of the grandeur of it than words are able to exprefs. Through this gate we pafs into a vaft open hall, which rifes in a dome nearly to the top of the building. This hall was, by the order of the Emperor

Jehanguire, the fon of Acbar, highly decorated with painting and gilding; but in the lapfe of time it was found to be gone greatly to decay; and the Emperor Aurungzebe, either from fuperftition or avarice, ordered it to be entirely defaced, and the walls whitened. From this hall, through a fimilar arch to that in the front, we defcend into the garden; and the whole of the tomb difplays itfelf through an avenue of lofty trees. This avenue is paved with ftone: in the center is a large fquare bafon, which was formerly filled with water, but was quite dry when I faw it. In the center of the bafon was a fountain, the pipe only remaining: the fupply of water, indeed, had apparently been confiderable here, for all through the middle of the avenue, and on either fide, we obferved channels, which muft have been defigned for aqueducts, but which were then dry. At fome fmall diftance from the principal building rifes a high open gate, entirely of white marble, of exquifite beauty.

A BLAZING eaftern fun fhining full on this building, compofed of fuch varied materials, produces a glare of fplendour almoft beyond the imagination of an inhabitant of thefe northern climates to conceive; and the prefent folitude that reigns over the whole of the neglected garden, excites involuntarily a melancholy penfivenefs. After viewing this monument of an Emperor, whofe great actions have refounded through the world, and whofe liberality and humanity were his higheft praife, I became defirous of feeing even that ftone which contained his crumbling remains. There was an old Mollah who attended, and had the keys of the interior of the building, (which is ſtill held in veneration) and who obtains a precarious ſubſiſtence by ſhewing it to the curious traveller. The inſide of the tomb is a vaſt hall, occupying the whole ſpace of the interior of the building, which terminates in a dome; a few windows at the top admit a " dim religious" light, and the whole is lined with white marble. In the center the body is depoſited in a ſarcophagus of plain white marble, on which is written, in black marble inlaid, ſimply the name of

ACBAR.

FROM the ſummit of the minarets in the front a ſpectator's eye may range over a prodigious circuit of country, not leſs than thirty miles in a direct line, the whole of which is flat, and filled with ruins of ancient grandeur: the river Jumna is ſeen at ſome diſtance, and the glittering towers of Agra. This fine country exhibits, in its preſent ſtate, a melancholy proof of the conſequences of a bad government, of wild ambition, and the horrors attending civil diſſentions; for when the governors of this country were in plenitude of power, and exerciſed their rights with wiſdom, from the excellence of its climate, with ſome degree of induſtry, it muſt have been a perfect garden; but now all is deſolation and ſilence. Surrounding the monument of Acbar are many tombs; some of them very beautiful: most probably they cover the remains of certain branches of his family. The traditionary report is here, that they are the tombs of his wives.

On the high road from Agra to Dehli there are many small buildings, the form of which is a square pedestal, upon which rises a cone, to the heighth of about eight feet. In this cone there are a great number of square niches, in which were placed the heads of malefactors, in terrorem. These likewise served the purpose of marking the coss distances on the road: many of them are now broken down and covered in the dust.

To the south-east of the city of Agra is a beautiful monument, raised by the Emperor Shah Iehan for his beloved wife Taje Mahel, whose name it bears, and is called, by way of eminence, the Taje Mahel. It now stands two miles from the city, though formerly it joined it. Adjacent to this monument there was a great bazar, or market for the richest manufactures of India, and of foreign countries,* composed of six courts, and encompassed with great open porticoes; but scarcely a vestige of this building is now remaining. The Taje Mahel rises immediately from the river, founded on a base of red free-stone, at the extremity of which are octagon pavilions, consisting of

* See Tavernier

three ſtories each. On the ſame baſe are two large buildings, one on either ſide, and perfectly ſimilar, each crowned with three domes of white marble; the center dome conſiderably larger than the others. One of theſe buildings is a musjiid, or moſque; the other was deſigned for the repoſe of any great perſonage, who might come either on a pilgrimage to the tomb, or to ſatisfy a well-directed curioſity. On this baſe of free-ſtone (having a platform at leaſt of twenty-five feet in breadth) another reſts of white marble, of a ſquare form, and which is about fourteen feet high; the angles are octagon, from which riſe minarets, or vaſt columns tapering upwards, having three ſeveral galleries running round them, and on the top of each an open pavilion, crowned with a dome. Theſe minarets too, I ſhould have remarked, are of white marble, and contain ſtair-caſes which lead to the top. From this magnificent baſe, like thoſe already deſcribed, riſes the body of the building, which has a platform ſimilar to the above. The plan of this is octagon; the four principal ſides oppoſed to the cardinal points of the compaſs. In the center of each of the four ſides there is raiſed a vaſt and pointed arch, like that deſcribed in the gate of the tomb of Acbar; and the top above this arch riſes conſiderably higher than the other parts of the building. Thoſe faces of the building which form the octagon on either ſide the great arches, have two ſtories of pointed arches, with receſſes, and a low balluſtrade in front; the ſpandels above the arches are greatly enriched with different coloured marble inlaid: the heads of the arches within the recesses are likewise most highly enriched in the same manner: within the several arches running round the building are windows, formed by an open fret-work in the solid slab, to give light to the interior of the building. From behind this octagon front, and rising considerably higher, are four octangular pavilions, with domes. From the center of the whole, rising as high as the domes of the pavilions, is a cone, whence springs the great dome, swelling from its base outwards considerably, and with a beautiful curve finishing in the upper point of the cullus, on which rest two balls of copper gilt, one above the other: above the balls is a crescent, from the center of which a spear head terminates the whole. Each face of this building is a counterpart to the other, and all are equally finished.

WHEN this building is viewed from the opposite side of the river, it possesses a degree of beauty, from the perfection of the materials and from the excellence of the workmanship, which is only surpassed by its grandeur, extent, and general magnificence. The basest material that enters into this center part of it is white marble, and the ornaments are of various coloured marbles, in which there is no glitter: the whole together appears like a most perfect pearl on an azure ground. The effect is such as, I confess, I never experienced from any work of art. The fine materials, the beautiful forms, and the symmetry of the whole, with the judicious choice of situation, far surpasses any thing I ever beheld.

It was the intention of the royal founder to have erected on the opposite shore a similar building, for his own interment, and to have joined them by a marble bridge. This magnificent idea was frustrated by sickness, and by the subsequent disputes concerning the succession between his sons, and at last by his own imprisonment by Aurungzebe.

The garden, in which the Taje Mahel is situated, is entered from the opposite side, through a large and handsome gate of red free-stone, whence proceeds a large flight of steps into the garden. From the top of the steps the center part of the middle building is viewed through an avenue of cypress and other trees mixed: the avenue is paved with stone, in the middle there are copartments, or beds of flowers, with fountains at equal distances; four of the most magnificent of which are situated about half way up the avenue, and rise from a square base of white marble. These, as well as the others, are supplied by a reservoir without the building, which is filled from the river by pumps. The fountains are yet in tolerable repair; they were played whilst I was there; and the garden is still kept in decent order, the lands allotted for the support of the building not being wholly dismembered from it. The center building is in a perfect state; but all those which surround it bear strong marks of decay. Several Mollahs attend the mofque here at the hours of prayer, and appear the moſt orderly and decent that I have ſeen among the Mahomedans; extremely attentive to ſtrangers, and aſſiduous to ſhew and explain every part of it. The inſide of the great building is of white marble, with many ornaments of flowers beautifully carved. The tomb is in a chamber below, and the body of Taje Mahel lies in a ſarcophagus of white marble, under the center of the building. Cloſe to it is a ſimilar one, containing the body of her huſband Shah Iehan. Theſe ſarcophagi are perfectly ſimilar to thoſe in the tomb of Acbar.

THE garden and the ſurrounding buildings cannot occupy a ſpace more than equal to one half of that of the Emperor Acbar, at Secundrii. Tavernier mentions, that he was witneſs to the beginning and the finiſhing of this building, which employed upwards of twenty thouſand men conſtantly at work for a term of twenty-two years. The free-ſtone was obtained in the neighbourhood, but the marble was brought from Kandahar, the eaſtern province of Perſia, by land carriage, a diſtance of not leſs than ſix hundred miles by the road. The expence is ſaid to have amounted to little leſs than one million ſterling.

ON the third of March the Nabob's camp moved cloſe to Secundrii, where we remained until the fifteenth, when we removed to Gougaut, ſeven cofs from Agra. Here the

A WOMAN of HINDOSTAN.   MULLAH or MUSSELMAN PRIEST.

Engraved by P. W. Tomkins, from a Drawing
made from the Life, by W. Hodges R.A.

London, Published by J. Edwards, Pall Mall, Jan. 1.1793.

water was very bad, being ſtrongly impregnated with nitre, and the ſurface of the ground was covered with that ſalt. On the twenty-ſecond we encamped near the ſmall village of Krowley, five coſs to the weſtward of Gougaut, on a very extenſive plain, which was poorly decorated with a few ſcattered trees, and bounded by ſome low hills ſtretching to the eaſtward. In theſe hills I found conſiderable quarries of red free-ſtone, the ſame with that of which the fort of Agra is built. The ground was very little cultivated in theſe parts: the ſoil is looſe and light.

I FOUND the heat about this time exceſſive, and it was ſoon much increaſed by the ſetting in of the hot winds from the weſtward. The water through the whole of this part of the country is very bad, from the ſalt-petre.

ON the 23d we encamped near the town of Futtypoor Sicri. The country here reſembled, in moſt reſpects, that which we had juſt paſt. It is an immenſe plain, bounded to the ſouthward by a range of hills; not a ſhrub was to be ſeen; and the heat ſtill continued to increaſe. The ſoil, I obſerved was light, and almoſt as fine as hair-powder. It is impoſſible to deſcribe the diſagreeable effects which this circumſtance produces, when this fine duſt is taken up by the hot winds from the weſtward: the indifferent water too, with which the whole country abounds, muſt neceſſarily render the ſituation unhealthy.

I was much entertained, during our several marches, by the variety of characters I saw; the people of the bazar (the market) with their wives and children; the cavalry, who were continually manifesting their dexterity, in the oriental manner, by setting off their horses in full speed, firing behind, as if pursued by an enemy, and then instantaneously stopping, and flying back with the same velocity as they advanced, to the great terror of the poor people in their way. Their adroitness in the management of their horses is, indeed, wonderful; though, from the appearance of the animals, one would doubt whether they were able to move five miles.

To these I may add the majestic movements of the elephants; not only of those which carried the great men, but of those with the heavy baggage. The appearance, indeed, of the whole army, with the camels, artillery and baggage cattle, formed a scene highly gratifying to the mind, entirely new to a European, of singular variety, and even sublime. I could not, however, but observe the great apparent want of order in the line of march; not that my knowledge of the military art was sufficient to qualify me for passing a decided judgment; but the order I had seen in the camp under Sir Eyre Coote, in the Carnatic, and when those troops marched towards the enemy, gave me very different impressions from that which was now before me.

The town of Futtypoor Sicri, which lay under the hills I have before mentioned, is confiderable, and the country immediately near it is in tolerable cultivation. On the fummit of the higheft hill is a large mofque, which was built by Acbar. The building is in a high ftyle of Moorifh architecture. The afcent from the foot of the hill is by a flight of broad fteps, extending to the principal entrance, which is through a portal of great magnificence. After this we enter a large fquare, paved throughout, in which is the mofque, and round the fides are apartments for the different priefts. At the foot of the hill on which the mofque is fituated are the remains of the palace, occupying a great extent of ground. The palace is in total ruin, not a fingle apartment remaining; and the only part which ferves to give any idea of its former beauty is the principal gate. At the back of the hills on which the mofque and palace are built, was a lake, formed by great mounds of earth, artificially raifed to keep in the water, on which, when the palace was inhabited, a number of fine boats were kept of every defcription, for the entertainment of the Imperial Family. The boundaries and banks of the lake are now only to be traced, many parts of it being not only quite dry, but in actual cultivation. Throughout this part of the country the water is very bad, except at the mofque, where it is quite the contrary, the wells being funk confiderably lower than ufual, in fact, below the depth where the falt-petre is generated. While we continued here our feelings informed us of a confiderable increafe in the heat of the weather, in the courfe of a few days.

WE remained at Futtypoor Sicri until the twenty-fixth, when the camp moved to Siedpoor, about feven cofs, or a little more. Here we found the face of the country greatly altered; we marched through a territory in many parts well cultivated: to the S. W. of the village it is, indeed, extremely beautiful, being varied with hills, the vallies and plains between which were in fine cultivation. The village itfelf had been but a few months before plundered and burnt, and all the inhabitants maffacred, by Mahommed Beg Khawn, one of thofe chiefs who difputed for the fovereignty under the Great Mogul, on the death of Nudjiif Khawn, and who, a fhort time after, affaffinated with his own hand, in a friendly meeting, the chief of this army, Mirza Shuffy Khawn; and for thefe and many fimilar crimes fuffered death, by the order of Madajee Scindia, the Mahratta chief.

WE experienced great inconvenience about this time from the hot winds, as the reader may well conceive, when he is informed that, in the middle of the day, Farenheit's thermometer ftood in the fhade at 106. The great quantities of fand alfo raifed by the wind prevented us from feeing the fun fet for many days, the atmofphere for many degrees above the horizon being totally obfcured by the floating maffes of fand. During my ftay at Siedpoor there were feveral ftorms of wind only; arifing in the north-eaft quarter, and veering about until it fettled in the fouth-weft. The country people call them aundees, and typhawns; but while they rage they may well be called hurricanes; deftroying every thing in their courfe, and being accompanied with fuch quantities of duft, as to have the appearance of a moving cavern approaching to overwhelm the affrighted fpectators. In one of thefe ftorms of wind not a fingle tent in the whole camp was left ftanding. The duft raifed by the ftorm approaches with a wave-like motion, and affords a clear idea of thofe tempefts which are faid to happen on the plains of Arabia and in Africa, and which are fo admirably defcribed by Lucan; and after him by Mr. Addifon:

> Sudden th' impetuous hurricanes defcend,
> Wheel through the air, in circling eddies play,
> Tear up the fands, and fweep whole plains away.
> The helplefs traveller, with wild furprize,
> Sees the dry defert all around him rife,
> And, fmother'd in the dufty whirlwind, dies.

THE reader will perhaps have pleafure in comparing thefe with the following lines of Thomfon:

> Strait the fands,
> Commov'd around, in gathering eddies play:
> Nearer and nearer, ftill they dark'ning come;
> Till, with the general all-involving ftorm
> Swept up, the whole continuous wilds arife:
> And, by their noon-day fount dejected thrown,
> Or funk at night in fad difaft'rous fleep
> Beneath defcending hills, the caravan
> Is buried deep.

My intentions of visiting Dehli were frustrated by the movements of the army under Mirza Shuffy Khawn; and as no probability appeared of reaching that capital under the sanction of Major Brown's embassy, and the country being over-run by two hostile armies, as well as by marauding parties from each, and invaded by the Sciks from the province of Lahore, I was obliged in prudence to direct my course towards Gwalior. I therefore sent off all my baggage under the escort of a party of seapoys, and took my leave of Major Brown on the 28th of April, at night. Added to the evils which I intimated above, the whole country was at this time infested by bands of robbers; and during the march of my small party they were attacked by a considerable body of horsemen, but by the good conduct of the havildar every thing was preserved. On the 29th I arrived at the village of Dohlpoor, and on the following day crossed the river Chumbull, and marched three cofs, in a north-west direction, through the worst country I ever saw; full of ravines and deep hollow-ways. As soon as I reached the plain I encamped under the walls of a large mud fort, which had been lately taken from the Rana of Ghod, by Madajee Scindia, the Mahratta chief. The Killidar, or governor, treated my people extremely well, and permitted them to purchase grain and vegetables within the fort, but would not suffer me to enter it.

THE country through which I had lately paffed was moft dreary and defolate, not a blade of verdure to be any where feen, and the fun moft intenfely hot. On the 1ft of May I arrived at Nurabad. This is a fmall town, with an old ftone fort in it, and a ftone bridge over a fmall nullah, (a branch of the Chumbull) confifting of feven tall and narrow pointed arches: at the extreme of the three center arches are two open pavilions, raifed upon the bridge, crowned with domes on each fide; and at the extremes of the other two arches are fmall cones, all built of the fame ftone as the bridge, and finifhed with little domes: the remaining part of the bridge abuts againft the banks., On the following day I arrived at Gwalior.

I SHOULD have remarked, that throughout the whole of the above country, which I paffed in my way from Dohlpoor, there did not appear the fmalleft trace of cultivation, nor was there even a hut to be feen. The feafon, it is true, was the worft in the year for the appearance of the country, and the hot winds had fet in with uncommon violence, which deftroy every thing in their courfe, like the Angel of Defolation. Befides all thefe unfavourable circumftances, it muft alfo be remembered, that this is the bordering country, which lies between the fine province of Malwa and that country yet remaining under the dominion of the Great Mogul; and it has confequently been, ever fince the eftablifhment of the Mahratta power, the fcene of perpetual wars.

THE fort of Gwalior is feated on the top of a confiderable mountain, rifing from a perfect flat country. To the weft are fome confiderable hills, among which is the pafs of Narwah, leading to Ougion, the capital of the Malwah country, at prefent poffeffed by Madajee Scindia. The rock on which the fort is fituated is on every fide perpendicular, either by nature or art. At the north-weft end is the citadel and a palace, and a chain of feven gates leading to the town at the foot of the mountain. The town, and indeed the whole bafe of the mountain, is furrounded by a wall; and the place has been generally confidered, by Europeans, as the Gibraltar of the Eaft, as well for its natural fituation as for the works that have been conftructed for its fecurity. The town is large, and contains fome few remains of good houfes, and a mofque.

DURING the time of the Mogul government this place was the ftate prifon, where the obnoxious branches of the Royal Family were always confined, and where they were allowed, for their amufement, a large menagerie of beafts, fuch as lions, tigers, &c. On the top of the mountain, I am told, there are confiderable cultivated plains, and a good fupply of water; infomuch, that a vigilant and active governor might defend it againft almoft any number of enemies, who could only attack it from below.

THIS ancient and celebrated fortrefs is fituated in the heart of Hindoftan Proper, being about eighty miles to the fouth of Agra, the ancient capital of the empire, and one hundred and thirty from the neareft part of the Ganges. From Calcutta it is, by the neareft route, upwards of eight hundred miles; nine hundred and ten by the ordinary road; and about two hundred and eighty from the Britifh frontiers. In the ancient divifion of the empire it is claffed in the fubah of Agra, and is often mentioned in hiftory as the capital of a diftrict which produced a large revenue. We firft read of it in the Hiftory of Hindoftan, in the year 1008; and, during the two following centuries, it was twice reduced by famine. It is probable that it muft, in all ages, have been a military poft of the utmoft confequence, both from its fituation in refpect to the capital, and from the peculiarity of its fcite, which was generally deemed impregnable. With refpect to its relative pofition, it muft be confidered, that it ftands on the principal road, leading from Agra to Malwa, Guzerat, and the Decan; and that near the place where it enters the hilly tract, which advances from Bundelcund, Malwa, and Agimere, to a parallel with the river Jumna, throughout the greateft part of its courfe. From thefe circumftances, as well as from its natural and acquired advantages as a fortrefs, the poffeffion of it was deemed as neceffary to the ruling emperors of Hindoftan, as Dover Caftle might be to the Saxon and Norman Kings of England.

On the difmemberment of the Mogul empire, Gwalior appears to have fallen to the lot of a Rajah of the Jaut tribe of Hindoos, who affumed the government of the diftrict in which it is immediately fituated, under the title of Rana of Gohud or Gohd. Since that period it has changed mafters more than once: the Maharattas, whofe dominions extend to the neighbourhood of it, having fometimes poffeffed it, and, at other times, the Rana; but the means of transfer were always either by famine or treachery.

Gwalior was in the poffeffion of Madajee Scindia in the year 1779; at the clofe of which year the Governor General and Council of Bengal concluded an alliance with the Rana of Gohd; in confequence of which, four battalions of Seapoys, of five hundred men each, and fome pieces of artillery, were fent to his affiftance, his diftrict being over-run by the Maharattas, and he himfelf fhut up in his fortrefs of Gohd. The grand object of this alliance was to penetrate into Scindia's country, and finally to draw him from the weftern fide of India, where he then was, attending the motions of General Goddard, who was employed in the reduction of Guzerat. In adopting this meafure, the idea of Mr. Haftings was, that when Scindia found his own dominions in danger, he would detach himfelf from the confederacy, of which he was the principal member, and thus leave matters open for an accommodation with the court of Poonah, the principal feat of the Maharatta government; and the event was anfwerable to this expectation. Major, now Colonel Popham, was appointed to the command of this little army, fent to the Rana's affiftance, and was very fuccefsful, as well in clearing the country of the enemy, as in expelling them from one of their moft valuable diftricts, and keeping poffeffion of it. Mr. Haftings, who juftly concluded that the capture of Gwalior, if practicable, would not only open the way into Scindia's country, but would alfo add to the reputation of the Britifh arms, in a degree much beyond the rifque and expence of the undertaking, repeatedly expreffed his opinion to Major Popham, together with a wifh that it might be attempted; and founding his hopes of fuccefs on the confidence that the garrifon would probably have in the natural ftrength of the place, it was determined that it fhould be attacked. As the fuccefs, therefore, of this enterprize is only generally known, I have added the following account of the manner of obtaining poffeffion of it, from a letter written by Captain Jonathan Scott, at that time Perfian interpreter to Major Popham, to his brother Major John Scott, who has obligingly permitted the infertion of it in this work:

" THE fortrefs of Gwalior ftands on a vaft rock of about four miles in length; but narrow, and of unequal breadth, and nearly flat on the top. The fides are fo fteep, as to appear almoft perpendicular in every part; for where it was not naturally fo, it has been fcraped away; and the height, from the plain below, is from two hundred to three hundred feet. The rampart conforms to the edge of the precipice all round, and the only entrance is by fteps running up the fide of the rock, defended on the fide next the country by a wall and baftions, and farther guarded by feven ftone gateways, at certain diftances from each other. The area within is full of noble buildings, refervoirs of water, wells, and cultivated land; fo that it is really a little diftrict in itfelf. At the north-weft foot of the mountain is the town, pretty large, well built, the houfes all of ftone. To have befieged this place would have been vain; for nothing but a furprize or blockade could have carried it.

"A TRIBE of banditti, from the diftrict of the Rana, had been accuftomed to rob about this town, and once in the dead of night had climbed up the rock, and got into the fort. This intelligence they had communicated to the Rana, who often thought of availing himfelf of it, but was fearful of undertaking an enterprize of fuch moment with his own troops. At length he informed Major Popham of it, who fent a party of the robbers to conduct fome of his own fpies to the fpot: they accordingly climbed up in the night, and found that the guards generally went to fleep after their rounds. Major Popham now ordered ladders to be made, but with fo much fecrefy, that, until the night of the furprize, only myfelf and a few others knew of it.

"On the 3d of Auguft, in the evening, a party was ordered to be in readinefs to march, under the command of Captain William Bruce; and Major Popham put himfelf at the head of two battalions, which were immediately to follow the ftorming party. To prevent, as much as poffible, any noife in approaching or afcending the rock, a kind of fhoes, of woollen cloth, were made for the Seapoys, and ftuffed with cotton. At eleven o'clock the whole detachment moved from the camp at Reypoor, eight miles from Gwalior, through unfrequented paths, and reached it a little before day-break. Juft as Capt. Bruce arrived at the foot of the rock, he faw the lights which accompanied the rounds moving along the ramparts, and heard the centinels cough (the mode of fignifying that all is well in an Indian camp or garrifon), which might have damped the fpirits of many men, but ferved only to infpire him with more confidence, as the moment for action, that is, the interval between the paffing of the rounds was now afcertained: accordingly, when the lights were gone, the wooden ladders were placed againft the rock, and one of the robbers firft mounted, and returned with an account that the guard was retired to fleep. Lieutenant Cameron, our engineer, next mounted, and tied a rope ladder to the battlement of the wall; this kind of ladder being the only one adapted to the purpofe of fcaling the wall in a body (the wooden ones only ferving to afcend the crag of the rock, and to affift in fixing the rope ladder). When all was ready, Captain Bruce, with twenty Seapoy grenadiers, affembled without being difcovered, and fquatted down under the parapet; but, before a reinforcement arrived, three of the party had fo little recollection as to fire on fome of the garrifon, who happened to be lying afleep near them; this had nearly ruined the whole plan: the garrifon were of courfe alarmed, and ran in great numbers towards the place; but, ignorant of the ftrength of the affailants (as the men fired on had been killed outright), they fuffered themfelves to be ftopped by the warm fire kept up by the fmall party of grenadiers, until Major Popham himfelf, with a confiderable reinforcement, came to their aid. The garrifon then retreated to the inner buildings, and difcharged a few rockets, but foon afterwards retreated precipitately through the gate; whilft the principal officers, thus deferted, affembled together in one houfe, and hung out a white flag. Major Popham fent an officer to give them affurance of quarter and protection; and thus, in the fpace of two hours, this important and aftonifhing fortrefs was completely in our poffeffion: we had only twenty men wounded, and none killed. On the fide of the enemy, Bapogee, the Governor, was killed, and moft of the principal officers were wounded."

A VIEW of the FORT of GWALIOR.

It is neceſſary to add to this account, that ſome time after, the fort was given up to the Rana of Gohd, who kept poſſeſſion of it until the time of which I am now ſpeaking; the peace being agreed on between the Britiſh Government and Scindia, although not finally ſettled, that chief found himſelf at leiſure to inveſt it once more, and was at this time before the place with ſeventy thouſand men: he, however, only effected its reduction by the treachery of one of the Rana's officers, who admitted a party of the Maharatta troops. A view of Gwalior is given, taken on that ſide where the Engliſh troops eſcaladed, which was near the centre of the length of the mountain.

It would be the height of ingratitude not to make my acknowledgments, in this place, to Meſſrs. Anderſons, who were then in Scindia's camp, forming the treaty of peace and alliance between the Engliſh Company and Madajee Scindia, and which was afterwards ſo ably concluded by thoſe gentlemen, for the uncommon attentions I there received. Mr. Anderſon had ſent an eſcort of Maharatta horſe to Dohlpoor for my protection, which was abſolutely neceſſary, from the then ſtate of the country.

From the fatigue I had undergone, from the violent heats and expoſure to the ſun, in making my drawings, I found myſelf about this time, as indeed I had been for ſome time back, in a very indifferent state of health; nor was I able to stir abroad for many days after my arrival at Gwalior: in short, when I was, I was prevented from visiting the camp of the Maharattas, since the peace not being fully adjusted, many suspicions might have arisen to retard what was now so ardently desired, these people not having the remotest idea of any person visiting countries for scientific information, in any line whatsoever. After remaining ten days, I therefore determined to pursue my journey, with all expedition, to Lucknow; and accordingly proceeded by Dauk Bearers, and left my servants, with my baggage, to follow at leisure.

I SET off on the 12th, at night, and reached Gohd on the following day, where I stopped a few hours to refresh myself: here I found an Englishman, who was a watchmaker, but at this time commanded two battalions of the Rana's infantry; he expressed himself heartily tired of his military career, and a wish to return within the British territory, to his former occupation, as he had made some little property in the Rana's service, which he wished to retreat with, but had no means to convey it, not being suffered to depart; he therefore requested I would take charge of a casket for him to Lucknow, which I readily did, and delivered it to his friend. Had I, however, foreseen the dismal country I was to pass through, I should have been extremely averse to this undertaking; for, from the town of Gohd, it is hardly possible for the imagination to figure any thing fo difmal, dufky, and barren. There were no villages, and fcarcely a human being to be found, until I arrived near the river Chumbull, the banks of which are very high, and defcending through deep ravines, in fome of which are huts : in this part, as a ftranger paffes, every now and then a favage-like being ftarts out, completely armed in their way; fortunately, however, the countenance of an European is, in the prefent day, a paffport. I was two days and a night on this journey from Gwalior to Etaya. The heats, in the middle of the day were extreme, and the bearers, having one day miffed their way in this ocean of fand, they fet me down, and left me, while they went fome diftance to a hut to enquire the road. In this fituation I was for upwards of two hours, when fome of them returned; and heartily rejoiced I was at the fight of a human being: it was impoffible, indeed, to be angry at their long ftay, when I confidered what they muft have fuffered. On my arrival at Etaya, the fight of a few green herbs made me confider it as almoft a very Eden.

ON the 16th, I finifhed this journey at Lucknow, when the heats and fatigue I had fuffered brought on a violent dyfentery, and a palpitation at the heart, from which I was long in recovering. Colonel Polier received me with his wonted hofpitality; and I remained with that gentleman about ten days: my indifpofition, however, rather increafing than abating, his houſe being a large bungelow, * was conſequently very hot, and therefore Colonel Martin, who had a large brick houſe, had the goodneſs to invite me to his, where, by his great and moſt friendly care, and the adminiſtering of proper remedies, I gradually recovered; to him, therefore, I may now ſay I owe the life I at preſent enjoy.

I CANNOT but add, that, independent of this circumſtance, I feel a weight of obligations to that gentleman, for the many and repeated inſtances of his kind and friendly attention. During my ſtay in his houſe I painted ſeveral pictures, among others a large one, a View of the Palace of the Nabob, from which a print has been engraved, which is annexed.

* Bungelows are buildings in India, generally raiſed on a baſe of brick, one, two, or three feet from the ground, and confiſt only of one ſtory: the plan of them uſually is, a large room in the center for an eating and ſitting room, and rooms at each corner for ſleeping; the whole is covered with one general thatch, which comes low to each ſide: the ſpace between the angle rooms are viranders, or open porticoes, to ſit in during the evenings: the center hall is lighted from the ſides with windows, and a large door in the center; ſometimes the center viranders, at each end, are converted into rooms.

CHAP. VIII.

Departure from Lucknow—Voyage down the River Goomty—Danger from Banditti—Jionpoor—Mausoleum—Sasseram—Mausoleum of Shere Shah—Death of Mr. Cleveland—Arrival at Calcutta—Reflections on the State of the Arts in India—A new Project—Advice to Artists travelling in India.

FINDING myself tolerably recovered, I now determined to return towards Calcutta, and, instead of travelling the same rout by which I came, I resolved to pass by water down the river Goomty. I left Lucknow, therefore, on the 16th of July; and, from the various windings of the river, I did not enter the Ganges (into which the river falls) until the 1st of August.

THE banks of this river are, in most places, very beautiful, and at this season particularly so, having smooth, sloping banks of vegetable earth, and a fine verdure. There are many villages on its banks, between Lucknow and the town of Jionpoor, but less cultivation, than I should have judged, would have been necessary from the apparent population. It is somewhat dangerous to proceed down this river without an efcort of the military for protection: near the village of Sultanpoor, there appeared a body of about fifty horfe belonging to a famous marauder Rah Sing, who had made himfelf extremely obnoxious by his depredations. His party watched my boats the whole of one night, within fifty yards of us; the alertnefs of my Seapoys, however, prevented any attack, and at day-break the party marched off.

Not far from where this river enters the Ganges, ftands the fort of Jionpoor, a building of confiderable extent, on a high bank commanding the bridge. It is now chiefly in ruins, though formerly, from ftrength and natural fituation, it commanded the country from the Ganges quite to Lucknow: It was built by Sultan Feroz Shah, about the year 1102, and this place at one time was the feat of an empire. Chaja Jehan, Vizier to Sultan Mahummud Shah, during the minority of his fon, Sultan Mamood Shah, affumed the title of Sultan Shirki (or king of the Eaft), and took poffeffion of Bahar, and fixed his refidence at Jionpoor, where he built the great musjüd or maufoleum, which is ftill remaining, for the interment of himfelf and his family. This ruin is a great pyramid in the front, blunt at the top, the apex being cut off; the front is covered with ornaments. Over the center of the building in which are the remains of the tombs, rifes a dome, but much below the front of the building which is feen from without; there has alfo been a fquare of buildings in the front, as appears by the foundations, which now only remain.

THE bridge of stone crossing the Goomty at this place is in tolerable repair, and consists of sixteen pointed arches; on the top of the bridge are many little shops on both sides built of stone. From a Persian inscription on the bridge, we find it was founded by Khan Khannah, Vizier to the Emperor Acbar, and Subah of the province of Oud, in the year 1567. The sound principles upon which this bridge is built, are proved by its having withstood, for such a length of time, the force of the stream, which in the time of the rains is very great. The inundations have been frequently known to rise even over the bridge, insomuch, that in the year 1774, a whole brigade of the British forces passed over it in boats.*

THE river Goomty falls into the Ganges at a small distance below the city of Benares, whence I proceeded direct to Buxar. At this time I also determined to make a journey to Safferam, twenty cofs inland, the birth-place of the Emperor Shere Shah, to visit the mausoleum of that Emperor, and to make drawings of it. This being the season of the rains, it was with difficulty I could pass in my palankeen; in many places the bearers waded above their middle in water, and the whole ground was one continued swamp.

I COULD not but be greatly struck with the grandeur of this monument, rising from the center of a large square lake, each side bounded by masonry, and descending to the water by

* A brigade consists of ten thousand men.

stone steps on every side, now greatly ruined. I judged, by walking round the lake, and measuring it by time, to exceed a mile. The plan of this mausoleum is a square base, rising from the center of the lake, having at each angle pavilions crowned with domes, and finished with a cullus; from this base was a bridge, that, from the ruins now remaining, must have consisted of six pointed arches, which communicated to the side of the lake, and on two sides are a double flight of steps to the water; on the base is raised an octagon building, having three pointed arches in each face, and on each angle are pavilions finished like the former. Somewhat behind this runs an octagon with one window in each side, and on the angles, pavilions like the others below; behind this is likewise an octagon, ninety-two feet in diameter, and from the extremes spring the dome, which is finished on the top by a small pavilion, like those already described. A great part of the building is now covered with shrubs and trees, which have taken root within the stones, and promise a speedy decay, if not a total overthrow, of this grand pile. The country in the neighbourhood is hilly; and surrounding the lake are hills, formed by the excavations when it was first made; most of these are now covered with trees. The inside of the building is perfectly plain, nor does it appear ever to have had any decorations. The tomb of the Emperor is still remaining in the center, with several others surrounding it, which are those of his children. The dome, like the rest of the building, is of a fine grey free stone, now discoloured by age and neglect.

ON my return to Buxar, I proceeded to Bauglepoor, where I found my friend Mr. Cleveland on the bed of ficknefs, which in lefs than three months deprived the Indian world of his valuable life, a lofs irretrievable to his friends, and moft feverely felt by the public.

A CONSTANT, and indeed an inceffant application to public bufinefs, without fufficient care of a very delicate frame, and poftponing until it became too late, the expedient of trying a more favourable climate, terminated the mortal exiftence of this ineftimable man, who died on board a fhip, at the mouth of the Ganges, in which he had embarked for the Cape of Good Hope. His remains were brought back in the pilot vef-fel that had attended the fhip, and were afterwards depofited at Bauglepoor, where a handfome monument was erected to his memory.

I ARRIVED at Calcutta on the 24th of September, after a journey of nine months and fourteen days, through a country which had once been fubject to the Moguls; the greateft and the richeft empire, perhaps, of which the human annals can produce an inftance, and which was adorned by many really great characters in politics and in arms.

I CANNOT look back at the various fcenes through which I paffed in thefe excurfions, without almoft involuntarily indulging a train of reflections relative to the ftate of the arts, under this, as well as under the Hindoo government. The amazing monuments which are ſtill to be found in India, prove the Muſſulman conquerors, to have been well acquainted with the principles of architecture, and at leaſt to have had a taſte for grand compoſition ; in painting, on the contrary, they have only exerciſed themſelves in miniature, many of which are highly beautiful in compoſition and in delicacy of colour ; their attempts in this art have alſo been confined to water-colours ; and they have laboured under a further diſadvantage, the religion of Mahommed prohibiting all reſemblances of animated nature. Whether the Arabs have ever tranſgreſſed the law in this point, I know not; but probably, on account of the remoteneſs of India from the original ſeat of the religion of Mahomed, it may have loſt much of its rigour, and may, therefore, have left the princes of India at more liberty to indulge themſelves in this elegant art.

In ſculpture there are no inſtances of excellence among the Moors, except in the Taje Mahael at Agra, upon which there are flowers carved with conſiderable ability.

The Hindoos appear to me to riſe ſuperior to the Mahommedans in the ornamental parts of architecture. Some of the ſculptures in their buildings are very highly to be commended for the beauty of the execution; they may, indeed, be ſaid to be very finely drawn, and cut with a peculiar ſharpneſs. The inſtance which is produced in this work of a column from the

INDIA. 153

temple of Vis Vifha, at Benares, will prove it although cut in free-ftone. A fimilar inftance cut in black bafalt, in the collection of Charles Townley, Efq. (on which are ornaments fimilar to thofe which is referred to above) is a ftriking proof of their power in this art. This column was brought from Gour, an ancient city, (now totally demolifhed) fituated on the eaftern fhore of the Ganges, nearly oppofite to Rajemahel. I have feen many inftances of caft metal ftatues, relative to Hindoo mythology, that prove their perfect knowledge in the art of cafting. Thefe works, as they apply to the religion of Bramah, are both curious and valuable; but, as they are purely mythological, the artifts have only confidered the fymbolical character; without the proper attention, and, perhaps, without a power of giving a perfect beautiful form, fuch as we fee in the Grecian ftatues.

THE paintings of the Hindoos, as they are, like their fculpture, chiefly applied to reprefent the objects of their religious worfhip, are certainly not fo perfect as the Moorifh pictures, which are all portraits. A conftant ftudy of fimple nature, it is well known, will produce a refemblance which is fometimes aftonifhing, and which the painter of ideal objects never can arrive at.

I CANNOT clofe thefe pages without mentioning an intention which I entertained, after my laft journey, of undertaking another from the Ganges, through the Deccan, to the weſtern coaſt of India; and which I ſhould recommend to the attention of any artiſt who may be induced to viſit India, in future, with intentions ſimilar to thoſe which drew me from my native country. I meant to have commenced my journey at Benares, and finiſhed at Surat. As this is a part of India untrodden by an artiſt, much matter might be collected relative to the ſtate of ancient India, as many of the Rajahs in that part of the country poſſeſs lands handed down from the earlieſt period of the Hindoo records. I muſt think, from what I have ſeen of the Hindoo character, that ſuch a journey might be carried into execution with perfect ſafety, and would add greatly to our ſtock of knowledge relative to the Eaſtern continent.

It is but too true that the expences would be conſiderable, from the neceſſity of being attended by a great number of ſervants; for, as is juſtly obſerved by Mr. Orme, in his ſecond volume, " The different caſts of the Indian religion being appropriated to ſpecific and hereditary vocations, many of them are entirely prohibited from ſervile offices and hard labour; and of thoſe allotted to ſuch occupations, each muſt abide by that alone to which he was born: the huſbandman would be diſhonoured by employing his mattock, excepting in the field he is to ſow; and even lower races have their diſtinctions, inſomuch, that the cooly, who carries a burden on his head, will not carry it on his ſhoulder." The reputation, however, that would neceſſarily at-

INDIA. 155

tend the completion of such an undertaking, would be more gratifying than whatever wealth might be accumulated in the common track of professional pursuits.

A PAINTER for such pursuits ought necessarily to be endowed with three great qualities; a perfect knowledge of his art, and with powers to execute readily and correctly; judgment to chuse his subjects; and fancy to combine and dispose them to advantage. The first I must suppose him possessed of; in the second is included the choice of subject, with the knowledge of all the parts necessary for such a subject; and in the third is included the combination of all the different parts, so as to produce a general effect: but the imagination must be under the strict guidance of cool judgment, or we shall have fanciful representations instead of the truth, which, above all, must be the object of such researches. Every thing has a particular character, and certainly it is the finding out the real and natural character which is required; for should a painter be possessed of the talents of a Raphael, and were he to represent a Chinese with the beauty of a Grecian character and form, however excellent his work might be, it would still have no pretensions to reputation as characteristical of that nation.

MANY other tours in that interesting country might be undertaken by the enterprizing artist. We know that the whole coast of Malabar possesses picturesque beauty equal to any country on earth; and how valuable would be the reprefentation of that fcenery, whether as a natural objeƈt, or as conneƈted with the hiftory of the country, and the manners of the people? Piƈtures are colleƈted from their value as fpecimens of human excellence and genius exercifed in a fine art; and juftly are they fo: but I cannot help thinking, that they would rife ftill higher in eftimation, were they conneƈted with the hiftory of the various countries, and did they faithfully reprefent the manners of mankind.

FINIS.

www.ingramcontent.com/pod-product-compliance
Lightning Source LLC
Chambersburg PA
CBHW032135160426
43197CB00008B/655